The IU Cookbook

By Terry Murray

Hoosier Hearthside Cookery Series

Guild Press of Indiana, Inc.
6000 Sunset Lane
Indianapolis, Indiana 46208

The IU Cookbook

By Terry Murray

Library of Congress
Catalog Card Number
93-079619

ISBN 1-878208-33-0

 Published in the United States by Guild Press of Indiana, Inc.

Indiana University has not reviewed nor tested the individual recipes contained in this book, and takes no responsibility for their use in the preparation of any foods described herein.

Table of Contents

Acknowledgments

I take this opportunity to express sincerest gratitude to those individuals who have graciously contributed their favorite recipes toward the completion of this worthy project. And I thank you, the consumer, who in purchasing this book have automatically donated eight percent of the wholesale price towards academic and athletic scholarships awarded annually to Indiana University students!

T.M.

For Darrell
and Matthew

Introduction

George Bernard Shaw wrote, "There is no love sincerer than the love of food." Hoosiers love good food and are noted for good cooking and warm hospitality around the dinner table. These go hand in hand: good food, good friends, good cheer.

I came to the University when it was much smaller than it is now: smaller in area, smaller in student body, and smaller in faculty and staff. University events, however, have always been characterized by good food. Bean suppers before the Homecoming football games, picnics at alumni gatherings, barbecues to welcome new faculty, formal lunches and dinners to welcome special guests to the University or to entertain guests in our homes—all are welcome occasions in our lives in the University community.

When I go to the residence halls for dinner, I am always amazed at the variety and quality of the food. The dieticians and cooks make a great effort to vary their menus and make them attractive to the students. I think, by and large, they are successful. The fraternities and sororities also do a good job, sometimes at the expense of solvency, but nevertheless they provide well-prepared and well-served meals.

Present day Bloomington is noted for its ethnic restaurants, reflecting the diverse and interesting makeup of its citizens. Perhaps it has more different types of ethnic restaurants than any other city its size in Indiana. They are all patronized by a student body eager to learn something about foods of other cultures and regions.

In my travels I have had the good fortune to enjoy meals in many lands. It always is a pleasure for me to experience firsthand the hospitality of persons in other countries. But Hoosier food continues to be the best, as far as I am concerned. There is nothing quite like a good, home-cooked Hoosier meal.

Indiana University now has eight campuses. You will find in this book recipes from all of the campuses. I commend them to you. They are honest, and down-to-earth recipes which, if followed, will yield good results and, I hope, many hours of enjoyment and good cheer.

Herman B Wells
Chancellor, Indiana University
July 1993

Administrators
and others . . .

Chancellor Herman B Wells

Fresh Corn Pudding

8 ears of corn, cut off the cob (about 2 cups)
2 cups half-and-half
4 eggs, beaten
1 stick butter
1/2 cup sugar
8 drops Tabasco sauce

Heat half-and-half and butter; add sugar and Tabasco sauce. Add eggs to corn; stir into half-and-half mixture.

Pour into greased 2-quart casserole. Place casserole in pan of hot water.

Bake at 325° for one hour or until knife inserted in center comes out clean. Serves 8.

HERMAN B WELLS
Chancellor of Indiana University
Bloomington, Indiana

Broccoli Casserole

2 packages frozen chopped broccoli
1/2 pound Velveeta cheese (diced)
salt to taste
1 stick margarine
1/4 pound Ritz crackers

Cook broccoli and drain well. Combine with 1/2 stick margarine and stir in cheese. Mix 1/2 stick melted margarine with crushed Ritz crackers and spread over top of broccoli mixture. Bake at 350° for 25 minutes.

MARY JANE (SILVER) ANDIS ROBLING—*BS '63*
Physical Education Teacher
Evansville, Indiana

Lois' Raisin & Cinnamon Biscuits

1 1/2 cups flour
1/4 cup sugar
2 teaspoons baking powder
1/4 teaspoon salt
1/4 cup margarine
1/2 egg
1/2 cup buttermilk or sour milk
1/2 cup raisins
1 to 2 teaspoons cinnamon
2 teaspoons grated orange peel (optional)

for egg wash, beat together
1/2 egg
1/2 tablespoon milk

In large bowl, mix flour, sugar, baking powder, cinnamon, and salt. Using a pastry blender, cut in margarine until mixture resembles coarse meal. In small container, stir egg until mixed. Divide into two equal portions. In small bowl, beat 1/2 egg with buttermilk and then add to flour mixture. Stir in raisins and orange peel. Mix well. Divide dough into 9 equal balls. Flatten to discs 1/2 inch thick.

Place on ungreased baking sheet, brush lightly with egg wash.

Bake in 375° oven 15 to 20 minutes or until golden brown. Serve warm or at room temperature. Drizzle biscuits with powdered sugar mixed with milk if desired.

LOIS JOHNSON-VINING—*BGS '91*
President, Event Planning Services
Indianapolis, Indiana

"These two recipes (for Suisse und Sauer, and Pfinzel) were originally from my great-grandmother from northern Germany."

— P.J.I.

Suisse und Sauer (*Siss and Sour*)

Place 3–4 pound lean beef roast in dutch oven and cover with cold water. Bring to boil. Simmer 1 hour, continually skimming off fat.

Add after 1 hour
3 tablespoons molasses
3 tablespoons brown sugar
1/4 cup vinegar
3/4 cup large seedless raisins
1 teaspoon salt

Add a pinch each of
whole cloves
whole allspice
whole pepper

Continue simmering until meat is tender.

In separate pan, melt and brown 1 tablespoon butter. Add 1/4 cup flour and brown, stirring constantly. Gradually add half of liquid from meat. Stir until thickened. Add this to meat, stirring vigorously until thick and smooth. Serves 6.

PETER J. INEICH—*BA '77*
Professional Search Recruiter
Garland, Texas

Pfinzel (Dressing for Poultry)

giblets from chicken or turkey
1 pound ground pork
1/2 loaf (8–10 slices) dried bread
3 ounces seeded raisins (found at gourmet or natural food store)
1/4 teaspoon ground nutmeg
salt and pepper to taste

In food processor, grind giblets and add ground pork. Soak dried bread in water and squeeze out excess water. Break into pieces and add to meat mixture. Combine. Add remaining ingredients. Mix thoroughly and stuff bird. Roast until done.

PETER J. INEICH—*BA '77*
Professional Search Recruiter
Garland, Texas

Family Favorite

3 or 4 pound lean beef roast
2 teaspoons salt
1/4 teaspoon pepper
3 tablespoons oil
1/2 cup water
8 ounces tomato sauce
2 medium onions, sliced
2 cloves garlic, minced

Rub meat with salt and pepper, and brown in hot oil. Add water, tomato sauce, onions, and garlic. Cover and simmer 1 1/2 hours.

Combine the following and pour over meat:

2 tablespoons brown sugar
1/4 teaspoon paprika
1/2 teaspoon dry mustard
1 tablespoon Worchestershire sauce
1/4 cup catsup
1/4 cup vinegar
1/4 cup lemon juice

Continue cooking 1 hour. Remove meat, skim fat and thicken gravy. Serves 6.

(NOTE: To prepare in crock pot, do not brown meat; combine all ingredients and pour over meat. Cook on high 4 hours or low 8 hours.)

PETER J. INEICH—*BA '77*
Professional Search Recruiter
Garland, Texas

"This super-easy recipe is a year-round favorite and it freezes beautifully. It's great warm or cold (and holds together fine for milk dunking!)."

—J.S.

Apple Cake

2 eggs (Note: may use egg substitue for reduced fat)
2 cups sifted flour
2 teaspoons cinnamon
1/2 teaspoon salt (optional)
1 teaspoon baking soda
1 cup oil (for low fat, substitute 1 cup applesauce)
1 teaspoon vanilla
3/4 to 1 cup sugar (depends on tartness of apples)
4 cups thin sliced apples
nuts (optional)

Mix all ingredients well with spoon. Pour in greased and floured tube or bundt cake pan.

Bake 45-60 minutes at 350°

Optional Icing

3 ounces cream cheese, softened
3 tablespoons melted butter
1 teaspoon vanilla
1 1/2 cups powdered sugar

Mix with mixer and spread on cooled cake.

JEFF SLYN—*BS '79*
Micro computers sales & support
Louisville, Kentucky

"Fudge Squares and Tex-IU-Mex-IU Dip — these are recipes I use for IU tailgate parties, prior to home games in Bloomington."

—A.L.F.

Fudge Squares

1 cup margarine or butter
2 cups sugar
4 ounces unsweetened chocolate
4 eggs
1 cup flour
1/2 teaspoon salt
1 teaspoon vanilla

Melt butter or margarine in saucepan or in microwave in microwave-safe bowl. Melt chocolate, combine with butter or margarine; stir and cool. Add eggs and sugar. Mix well. Add salt and flour, stir; add vanilla. Spread in 9 x 13-inch baking pan.Sprinkle chopped nuts on top.

Bake in pre-heated oven for 30 minutes at 350°.

Cut into squares when cool. Should be fudgey, not cakey.

ANITA LINN FISHMAN—*BS '58*
Self-employed
South Bend, Indiana

Tex-IU-Mex-IU Dip

Serve this with tortilla chips.

Bottom layer

2 cans plain or jalapeño bean dip
(Note: I use refried beans without lard)

Middle layer

3 medium ripe avocados, chopped
2 tablespoons lemon juice
1/2 teaspoon salt
1/4 teaspoon pepper
(Blend middle layer ingredients in food processor)

Top layer

1 package taco mix, combined with
1 cup sour cream (may use reduced fat)
1/2 cup mayonnaise (may use reduced fat)

Top all with

8 ounces shredded cheddar cheese
3 medium tomatoes chopped
chopped ripe olives
chopped green onions

ANITA LINN FISHMAN—*BS '58*
Self-employed
South Bend, Indiana

"When time is short, this is a wonderful make-ahead meal!"

— R.R.E.

Bloomington Friends Barbecue Chicken on Rice

3 pounds chicken breasts, cut up
1/4 cup flour
1/2 teaspoon pepper
1/2 cup diced onion
1 cup diced green pepper
1 cup tomato juice
1/2 cup tomato puree
1/4 cup white vinegar
1 teaspoon chili pepper
1/2 cup oil
1 teaspoon salt
1/2 teaspoons paprika
1 cup diced celery
1/4 cup ketchup
1 teaspoon dry mustard
3 cups cooked rice

Mix flour, salt, pepper and paprika together. Roll chicken in mixture until coated. In skillet heat 1/2 cup oil and brown chicken on all sides. Remove and drain on paper towel.

In skillet add onion, celery, and green pepper; saute until light brown. Pour off any oil, add remaining ingredients and bring to boil. Lower heat and simmer for 10 minutes.

Place browned chicken into large ovensafe dish. Pour sauce over chicken. Place in refrigerator for 2 hours or more. Bake at 350° for 1 hour, covered. Serve with rice.

RICHARD R. EUBANK—*BS '60*
Retired
Evansville, Indiana

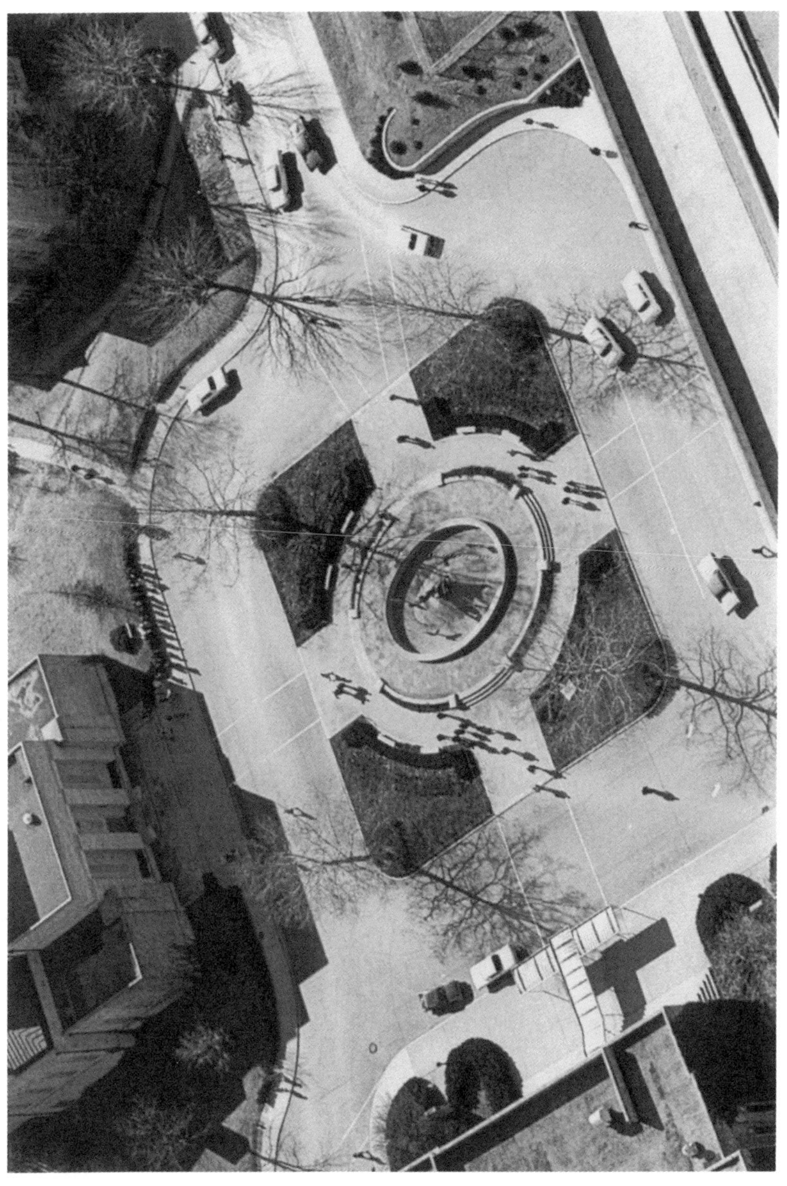

The Showalter Fountain on the Bloomington campus.

"This is easliy prepared before the game starts, and can be eaten with a salad during or after the game."

—P.W.B.

One Pan Lasagna

2 16-ounce jars spaghetti sauce
1 16-ounce box lasagna noodles
1 24-ounce container of cottage cheese or ricotta cheese
10 ounces shredded mozzarella cheese
1/2 cup grated parmesan cheese

Spray 13 x 9 x 2-inch pan with no-stick cooking spray. Cover bottom of baking dish with spaghetti sauce. Add layer of uncooked noodles on top of sauce. Spread half the ricotta cheese and half the mozzarella over noodles. Sprinkle 2 tablespoons parmesan over this. Add another layer of sauce. Repeat ricotta cheese and mozzarella and 2 tablespoons parmesan.

Top with layer of noodles. Pour remaining sauce over noodles.

Cover with foil. Bake 350° for 1 hour 15 minutes or until knife goes through pasta.

Place pan on cookie sheet in oven to catch spills.

PEGGY WELLER BAILEY—*MS '76*
Middle school teacher
Summitville, Indiana

Casserole Bread

1 package dry yeast
1/4 cup warm water (100-115°)
1 tablespoon butter or margarine, softened or melted
1 cup small-curd cottage cheese, room temperature
2 tablespoons sesame seed, caraway seed, or dill weed
2 tablespoons granulated sugar
1 teaspoon salt
1/4 teaspoon baking soda
1 egg
1 tablespoon minced onion, fresh or dehydrated
2 1/4 to 2 1/2 cups all-purpose flour

Dissolve the yeast in 1/4 cup warm water, in large mixing bowl. Add all remaining ingredients and mix well. The dough will be wet and sticky. Cover the bowl and let the dough rise in a warm place until double in bulk. Stir down the dough with a spoon and put it into a well-greased two quart casserole dish. Let rise 30-40 minutes.

Bake at 350° for 40-50 minutes, or until the loaf is well browned and sounds hollow when tapped. The loaf will appear bumpy and irregular on the outside, but has a wonderful color, texture and aroma when sliced.

ANDREA POLLEY BREWER—*MAT '79*
Speech pathologist
State College, Pennsylvania

Mrs. Gleich's Dump Cake

1. Lightly grease oblong 9 x 13-inch cake pan
2. "Dump" in 1 medium can chopped pineapple in unsweetened juice
3. "Dump" in 1 can cherry pie filling
4. "Dump" in 1 box vanilla cake mix
5. Cover with layer of finely chopped walnuts
6. Dot with butter pats
7. Bake at 350° for 1 hour, or until toothpick can cleanly be removed from center of cake.
8. Serve with whipped cream if desired.

(NOTE: flavors of cake mix and pie filling can be alternated.)

CYNTHIA GLEICH AGRESS—*BA '72*
Actress and teacher
Westfield, New Jersey

"Our family enjoys this best after cooling in the refrigerator. They like to add butter but it is also good alone. It can also be used like a cake and is excellent when spread with cream cheese frosting."

—M.A.S.

Poppy Seed Bread

4 eggs
1 cup liquid oil (may use 3/4 cup to decrease fat content)
2 cups sugar
3 cups flour
1 teaspoon vanilla
1 1/2 teaspoons baking soda
1 13-ounce can lowfat evaporated milk
1 teaspoon salt
5 tablespoons poppy seeds

Combine eggs, sugar, vanilla, baking soda and salt. Mix at low speed of mixer. Add oil and mix to blend. Alternate flour and evaporated milk while mixing at low speed of mixer. Stir in poppy seeds.

Spray two large loaf pans, or a bundt pan and one small loaf pan, with a nonstick cooking spray. Divide batter into prepared pans. Bake at 350° for one hour, if using bundt pan, or 40-50 minutes if using loaf pans.

Remove from pans after ten minutes and allow to cool.

MARCIA A. FEY SCHROEDER—*MS '81*
Physician consulting/lecturer
Lanesville, Indiana

Chinese New Year Cookies

1 6-ounce package semisweet chocolate bits
1 6-ounce package butterscotch bits
1 3-ounce can Chinese noodles
1 7 1/2-ounce can salted peanuts

In double boiler, melt chocolate and butterscotch pieces. Mix in noodles and nuts. Drop by teaspoon on to wax paper. Chill. Makes 4 dozen.

SANDRA SMITH DORSTE—*MAT '69*
Nightclub singer, commercial musician
Indianapolis, Indiana

Ham Loaf

1 1/2 pounds lean fresh pork
3/4 pound cured ham
1 small onion diced
3 eggs
1 cup bread crumbs
1 No. 2 can tomato juice
Pepper (to taste)

Soak crumbs in tomato juice to moisten Add meat, onion, eggs and pepper. Mix well. (If too dry add more tomato juice.) Pour into pan and shape into a loaf. Drizzle tomato juice over loaf. Bake in 350° for 45-50 minutes

Let stand 10 minutes before slicing.

(NOTE: To increase in size, use meat in proportion of 2-1. Good served with sour cream horseradish sauce.)

MIRIAM ELIZABETH SMALLWOOD—*MS '42*
Retired teacher
Oolitic, Indiana

"This favorite 'red and white' family recipe has been a Thanksgiving and Christmas tradition for forty years."
—G.R.

Creamy Cranberry Salad

1 pound chopped cranberries
1 cup sugar

Add sugar to chopped berries and let stand while combining other ingredients.

Combine with berry mixture
1 1/2 cups red grapes, cut up
1 1/2 cups mini-marshmallows

Combine last
1 cup walnuts, chopped
Whipped cream or prepared whipped topping

Mix well, put in square serving dish.
Cover dish and chill overnight.

Makes 9-10 servings.

GRACIA REID—*Ed D '78*
Elementary school principal
Merrillville, Indiana

"This recipe comes from my mother and the World War II era when eggs were scarce and food was rationed. It's a holiday tradition in our families."

—J.M.B.

Baked Chocolate Pudding Cake

No-egg batter—mix in a large bowl:

Sift:

1 cup flour
3/4 cup sugar
2 teaspoons baking powder
1/4 teaspoon salt
3 tablespoons cocoa
1/2 cup chopped walnuts

Add:

1/2 cup milk
2 tablespoons melted butter
1 teaspoon vanilla

Pour into a buttered 8 or 9-inch cake pan

Cake Topping—mix in a small bowl:

1/2 cup sugar
1/2 cup brown sugar
2 rounded teaspoons cocoa

Stir together with fork until mixed. Sprinkle the cake topping over the cake batter in the pan.

(NOTE: For ease in handling, place the pan containing the cake batter and topping on the oven rack prior to the next step.)

Pour 7/8 cup of boiling water over cake topping. DO NOT STIR.

Slide rack slowly into oven. Bake at 350° for about 40 minutes (do not overbake).

Remove cake from oven and *immediately* invert pan on a plate that is larger than cake pan. Tap bottom of pan to make sure cake slides out. Serve with whipped cream.

JOHN M. BRITT—*BGS '90*
Budget Administrator
Richland, Washington

Crabmeat Pizza

11 ounces cream cheese
6 1/2 ounce can fancy crabmeat
2 teaspoons Worcestershire sauce
2 teaspoons lemon juice
8 ounces chili sauce
2 tablespoons minced onion
fresh parsley, chopped

Cream together the cream cheese, onion, juice and Worcestershire sauce. Spread the mixture on a 12-inch plate so it resembles "pizza" dough. Spread on the chili sauce to within 3/4 inch of edge of plate. Sprinkle on the drained and flaked crabmeat. Sprinkle top lightly with parsley.

Refrigerate until it is served. Serve with crackers or raw vegetables.

SCOTT A. HICKS—*BS '89*
Sales Coordinator
Ligonier, Indiana

Noodle Hot Dish

1 pound ground beef
1 medium onion minced or 1/2 package onion soup mix
salt and pepper
dash of seasoned salt or garlic salt
1/4 ounce Old English Cheese (or about 6 slices)
4 ounces noodles
1 can tomato soup
1 small jar mushrooms and liquid

Saute beef and onion (don't brown).

Cook noodles

After hamburger is sauteed, combine all and simmer until cheese melts.

Add a half can of water

Stir and put in casserole dish.

Bake at 325° for 1 hour

CINDY HENDRICKS WILLIAMS—*AB '73*
Jury Clerk
Lutz (Hillsboro County) Florida

Christmas Fruit Salad

1 16-ounce can fruit cocktail
1 can peaches, drained and cut in cubes
2 or 3 bananas, diced
1 can pineapple tidbits, drained
red grapes, peeled and cut in half
1/2 teaspoon vanilla
2 or 3 tablespoons sugar
8 ounces (half pint) whipping cream

Mix first seven ingredients. Whip cream and fold into fruit.

CINDY HENDRICKS WILLIAMS—*AB '73*
Jury Clerk
Lutz (Hillsboro County) Florida

The Neighbor's Dessert

1 large can fruit pie filling, cherry, peach, or blueberry
1 large can crushed pineapple, drained
1 large tub whipped topping
1 can Eagle Brand Condensed milk

Mix all items together and refrigerate. This can also be frozen.

CINDY HENDRICKS WILLIAMS—*AB '73*
Jury Clerk
Lutz (Hillsboro County) Florida

"My wonderful godmother...made these soft ginger cookies for my two brothers and I....The mouth-watering smell of these cookies baking today brings back the memory of that loving woman in her large, warm Indiana farm kitchen, and three little devil boys waiting—and watching, seated at the kitchen table."

— P.T.L.

Little Devil Cookies

1/2 cup margarine
3/4 cup sugar
1 1/4 cup molasses
4 1/2 cups flour
1 medium size egg
1 cup boiling water
2 teaspoons baking soda
2 teaspoons ginger
1 teaspoon salt
1 teaspoon cinnamon
1 teaspoon nutmeg
1 teaspoon cloves

Combine margarine, sugar, egg and molasses. Add the dry ingredients before adding the boiling water . Beat until smooth.

Drop cookie batter with teaspoon onto a lightly greased baking sheet. Bake for 8 to 10 minutes in 400° preheated oven.

Frost cookies while still warm! (Frosting recipe follows.) Makes 6 1/2 to 7 dozen cookies.

Lemon Butter Frosting

2 cups powdered sugar
1 tablespoon butter
1 teaspoon lemon extract

Combine with 3 tablespoons of milk (or water). Beat until smooth.

PATRICK T. LAMEY—*AB '71*
Retired, General Motors Security Operations
Speedway, Indiana

20–20 Vision Carrot Cake

2 1/2 cups flour
1 1/2 cups sugar
1 1/2 teaspoons baking powder
1 1/2 teaspoons soda
2 teaspoons cinnamon
1 teaspoon salt
1 cup salad oil
3 eggs
2 carrots; finely shredded
1 8-ounce can crushed pineapple with syrup:
2 teaspoons vanilla
1 cup chopped walnuts

Sift together in large mixing bowl the flour, sugar, baking powder, soda cinnamon and salt. Add oil, eggs and carrots and pineapple and vanilla. Mix until moistened. Beat two minutes. Stir in nuts.

Bake in greased 9 x 13-inch pan at 350° for 35 minutes or until done. Let cool and frost with cream cheese icing.

Icing

2 3-ounce packages cream cheese, softened
2 tablespoons soft butter

2 teaspoons vanilla
3 cups confectioners sugar

Combine softened cream cheese, butter, vanilla and beat with mixer until smooth. Slowly add powdered sugar. Milk may be added if icing is too thick to spread. Top with chopped walnuts.

SANDI HULLINGER—*OD '77*
Optometrist
Bluffton, Indiana

Easy Fruit Dip

1 7-ounce jar marshmallow fluff
1 8-ounce package "light" cream cheese, softened
1 teaspoon grated orange rind

Combine marshmallow fluff and cream cheese in mixing bowl. Beat until smooth. Stir in orange rind. Makes 2 cups.

Chill at least 30 minutes prior to serving. Serve with your favorite assorted fruits. Especially good with bananas, strawberries, apples, kiwis and melons.

ELIZABETH A. GRIFFIN—*BS '85*
CPA
Tinley Park, Illinois

"This recipe is a family favorite—just serve with a tossed green salad and your meal is complete!"

— M.P.K.

Shepherd's Pie

1 1/2 pounds ground beef
6 medium potatoes
3/4 envelope dry onion soup mix
1 teaspoon dried beef bouillon
milk, butter, cheese, pepper, flour

Brown ground beef, drain, add soup mix, bouillon. Add 1 tablespoon flour, stir well. Add 1 cup water and simmer 20 minutes. Boil potatoes, drain, mash with milk and butter, whip. Transfer meat mixture to 11/2 quart casserole, top with whipped potatoes and sprinkle with 1 cup grated cheddar cheese.

Bake for approximately 30 minutes at 350°.

MARY PARKER KALLOK—*BS '72*
Homemaker
New Brighton, Minnesota

"This recipe can be used either as a salad or as a dessert. It's sure to become a favorite."

—M.P.K.

Raspberry Pretzel Dessert

1 1/2 cups crushed pretzel sticks
2 3-ounce packages raspberry gelatin
1/2 cup margarine, softened
2 10-ounce packages frozen raspberries
3/4 cups sugar
1 cup sugar
1 8-ounce package cream cheese, softened
2 cups boiling water
1 9-ounce tub whipped topping

Combine crushed pretzels, 3/4 cup sugar and margarine. Press into 9x13-inch pan. Bake at 350° for 5 minutes, no longer. Cool. Mix together well the cream cheese and 1 cup sugar. Add whipped topping. Mix well. Spread over cooled crust. Seal around edges well. Dissolve gelatin with 2 cups boiling water, stir well. Add partially thawed raspberries. Stir. Pour over whipped topping/ cream cheese mixture. Refrigerate 4 to 6 hours or overnight.

MARY PARKER KALLOK—*BS '72*
Homemaker
New Brighton, Minnesota

Turkey Tenderloin Marinade

3/4 cup vegetable oil
3/4 cup "lite" soy sauce
1 teaspoon onion powder
1 teaspoon rosemary, or substitute 3 teaspoons fine herbs
1 teaspoon basil

Combine above ingredients and pour over 4 tenderloins in long pan, marinate several hours or overnight. Place tenderloins on grill, basting after each turn. Grill 15 minutes or until desired doneness.

MARY PARKER KALLOK—*BS '72*
Homemaker
New Brighton, Minnesota

"Makes a delicious appetizer—the Muenster cheese adds a wonderful flavor."

—M.P.K.

Golden Cheese Wheel

1 package yeast
1 beaten egg
2/3 cup warm water
12 ounces shredded Muenster cheese
2 cups flour
2 tablespoons oil
1/2 cup snipped parsley
1/2 teaspoon sugar
1/2 teaspoon garlic salt

1/2 teaspoon salt
1/2 teaspoon black pepper
2 or 3 tablespoons sesame seeds

In bowl combine yeast and 2/3 cup warm water, add 1/2 teaspoon sugar, 1/2 teaspoon salt. Add 2 cups flour and 2 tablespoon oil. Mix well; place on floured surface and knead 5-8 minutes. Place dough in bowl, cover, let rise until doubled in size, divide dough in half let rest for 10 minutes. Roll half of dough to 13-inch circle, place on 12-inch pan. Mix cheese, parsley, salt and pepper together, sprinkle evenly over dough, roll second half of dough to 13-inch circle, place over cheese mixture, seal edges, crimping both edges of dough together. Bake at 400° for 20 minutes. Brush top with beaten egg, sprinkle with sesame seeds. Bake 12-15 minutes more. Remove from oven, let set for 5 minutes, cut into wedges with pizza cutter or knife.

MARY KALLOK—*BS '72*
Homemaker
New Brighton, Minnesota

"No need to chew this bite-size cookie—it melts in your mouth."

—B.F.S.

Norwegian Christmas Cookies

1 cup butter, at room temperature
1/3 cup powdered sugar
3/4 cup cornstarch
1/8 teaspoon almond extract

1 cup cake flour

Combine all ingredients to form a smooth dough. Refrigerate overnight. Shape into 60 small balls.
Bake at 350° on ungreased cookie sheet for 12-15 minutes.
Frost when cool.

Icing

1 cup powdered sugar
1 teaspoon soft butter
1 tablespoon lemon juice

Blend to spreading consistency, adding a little more lemon juice if needed. Ice cookies with this mixture.

BEVERLY FOOTE SHREINER—*MS '64*
Retired teacher
Tucson, Arizona

"Tender enough to cut with a fork..."

—B.F.S.

Slow-Cooked Beef Roast

Sirloin roast, cut in serving size pieces
1 teaspoon salt
1 teaspoon garlic salt
2 tablespoons red wine
1 teaspoon pepper
2 tablespoons Worcestershire sauce
2 tablespoons sugar
3 tablespoons flour
1 can beer

Brown meat in slow cooker. Combine other ingredients and pour over meat. Cook covered on low for 4-5 hours.

BEVERLY FOOTE SHREINER—*MS '64*
Retired teacher
Tucson, Arizona

Swedish Butter Cookies

2 sticks unsalted butter
1/2 cup sugar
2 cups flour
2 egg yolks
Raspberry jam

Cream butter and sugar. Add egg yolks and flour. Blend well. Chill dough. Make 36 balls, walnut sized. Place on greased cookie sheet. Dip small glass in sugar and press balls to 1/4 inch thick. Using a thimble, make an indentation in center of cookie. Fill in with jam.

Bake at 325° for 12–15 minutes.

Store or freeze in tightly covered container.

BEVERLY FOOTE SHREINER—*MS '64*
Retired teacher
Tucson, Arizona

"We've had this for Thanksgiving and Christmas for as long as I can remember!"

—K.S.K.

Schmidt's Cranberry Salad

1 6-ounce package orange gelatin
1 package unflavored gelatin
2 cups sugar
1 large can crushed pineapple, drained
16 ounces cranberries, ground
3 thick-skinned oranges, ground
3 apples, finely chopped

Dissolve the orange gelatin in 2 cups boiling water. Add 1 cup cold water. Mix 1 package unflavored gelatin with 1/4 cup cold water and add to hot mixture.

Add 2 cups sugar and drained pineapple. Run cranberries, oranges, and apples through food processor (or finely chop); add to gelatin mixture.

Chill. Serve when firm.

KATHY SCHMIDT KERSHNER—*MLS '73*
Youth Services Librarian
Bloomfield Township, Michigan

Grandma's Super Yummy Snacks

8 cups popped popcorn
3 cups Kix cereal
2 cups broken corn chips
1 pound white chocolate or almond bark

Melt chocolate in top of double boiler, or melt carefully in a bowl in a microwave oven.

Mix popcorn, Kix and corn chips together. Pour chocolate over mixture and mix well.

Spread on waxed paper to harden. Break apart and serve. Store in airtight container.

STEPHEN A. KERSHNER—*MLS '73*
Joint Library Director
Bloomfield Township, Michigan

"The original recipe was handwritten inside the cover of my great-grandmother's everyday cookbook—ingredients only. Preparation is something we learned how to do by watching grandmother or my mother."

—M.J.E.

Persimmon Pudding

2 cups persimmon pulp
1 1/2 cups flour
1 1/2 cups buttermilk
1/8 teaspoon salt
1/2 teaspoon cinnamon
1/2 stick butter
2 cups sugar
1 teaspoon soda
1 teaspoon baking powder
2 large eggs
1 teaspoon vanilla
1/4 cup cream

Melt butter in 9 x 13-inch baking dish (not aluminum) and set aside. Add sugar to pulp and mix with well-beaten eggs. Add soda to milk and stir into previous ingredients. Sift dry ingredients. Mix in final ingredients of vanilla, cinnamon and cream. Mix melted butter from baking dish.

Pour batter into baking dish and bake at 325° for 45 minutes or until firm.

Serve at room temperature topped with whipped cream.

MICHAEL J. ELLIS—*BA '72*
Bank branch manager
Jeffersonville, Indiana

"This soup has been a big hit on those cold and blustery Indiana evenings, especially when served with warm oatmeal-raisin muffins."

—V.S.E.

Cheese and Sausage Soup

4 cups water
2 cups diced potatoes
2 cups whole-kernel corn
2 cups chopped celery
2 cups chopped carrots
1 beef bouillon cube
1/2 teaspoon Tabasco sauce
1 pound Kielbasa sausage
1 pound Velveeta Cheese

Cut sausage into bite size pieces. In a large saucepan or dutch oven, combine all ingredients except cheese. Simmer for 1 to 2 hours, or until vegetables are done. Add cheese just before serving, but be sure the cheese is well blended in the soup.

This soup is even better the next day as leftovers, but do not boil when reheating.

VIRGINIA ANN SHRINER ENAS—*BSW '82, MSW '83*
Social worker
Indianapolis, Indiana

Meatloaf

1 pound hamburger
1 pound savory sage pork sausage
1 egg
1/2 to 3/4 cup ketchup
1 envelope onion-mushroom dry soup mix
handful of seasoned croutons

Mix all together, shape into loaf and bake at 350° for 1 hour. (NOTE: I cook this in a 9x13-inch roasting dish so that the meatloaf isn't sitting in all the grease.)

VIRGINIA ANN SHRINER ENAS—*MSW '83*
Psychiatric social worker
Indianapolis, Indiana

"The aroma of this hearty dish warms the house and welcomes you home on a chilly day."

—S.M.

Beef Burgundy

2 pounds round steak cut into 1-inch or smaller cubes (easier to cut if partially frozen)
5 carrots, cut up
2 medium onions, sliced into rings, cut and separated
2 cups (16 ounces) canned tomatoes
3/4 cup burgundy wine
1 8-ounce can tomato sauce
1/8 teaspoon garlic salt
3 tablespoons regular tapioca
2 tablespoons brown sugar
1 teaspoon salt
1/2 teaspoon pepper
4 to 5 potatoes

Combine everything except the potatoes in a large bowl and mix well. Pour into one large or two medium size deep casserole dishes. Bake at 250° for 4 hours.

Peel and cube potatoes and stir into the stew. Increase oven temperature to 300° and bake for 1 1/2 hours or until vegetables are tender.

Serves 6-8. Good reheated.

SUSIE MISHKIN—*BS '73*
Occupational Therapist
Kingsport, Tennessee

"Terrific for home parties for an IU game on TV."
—*R.K.B.*

Swiss Bacon Pleasers

Makes 24 appetizers

1 can (8 ounces) crescent dinner rolls
3 slices (7 x 4 inches) Swiss cheese
3 eggs, slightly beaten
3/4 cup milk
1 tablespoon instant minced onion or 1/4 cup chopped onion
6 slices bacon, fried and crumbled
1 tablespoon parsley flakes

Separate dough into 4 triangles. Place in bottom of ungreased 13 x 9-inch baking pan. Press over bottom and one inch up sides of pan to form a crust. Place cheese slices over dough.

In small mixing bowl, combine eggs, milk and onion; Pour over cheese slices. Sprinkle with crumbled bacon and parsley flakes.

Bake at 425° for 18-20 minutes.

Cool 5-10 minutes before cutting into squares. Serve warm or cold.

RUTH E. KINTZ BAHLER—*BSN '72*
Retired
Sebring, Florida

Bestyet

2 cups (1 box) brown sugar
3/4 cup butter (1 1/2 sticks) margarine
2 eggs
1 cup flour
1 teaspoon vanilla or hickory flavoring
1 cup nuts slightly chopped—pecans preferred

Melt sugar and butter together, but do not boil. Slightly beat the two eggs. Combine all ingredients and stir well. Spread the mixture in a greased 9 x 9-inch pan and bake at 350° for 45 to 50 minutes.

Allow to cool 15 minutes then cut into 1-inch squares.

JOSEPH F. TROSPER—*DBA '54*
Retired Professor
McKinney, Texas

Barbecue Cups

1 pound hamburger
3/4 cup barbecue sauce
2 teaspoons instant onion (optional)
dash garlic powder
refrigerator biscuits (12-count size)
4 ounces grated cheddar cheese

Brown beef, drain off fat. Add sauce, onion, garlic powder. Mix well. Flatten each biscuit and press into muffin tin. Spoon beef mixture into center of each muffin cup, top with cheese.

Bake at 400° for 10–12 minutes. Makes 12 servings. These are great to make ahead and reheat, wrapped in a napkin, in the microwave.

BOB PACE—*MS '86*
Teacher & Basketball Coach
Liberty Center, Indiana

Topsy's Cinnamon Diamonds

Cream together:
1 cup margarine or butter
1 cup brown sugar

Add:
1 egg yolk

Sift together and add to the above:
2 cups flour
1 tablespoon cinnamon

1 egg white
slivered almonds

Cream together first two ingredients. Add egg yolk. Sift flour and cinnamon. Add to creamed mixture.

Put dough into cookie pan. Brush with egg white. Cover with almond slivers.

Bake at 250° for 50 minutes and cut while warm.

THOMAS EHRLICH
President, Indiana University
Bloomington, Indiana

IU President Thomas Ehrlich

Political Figures, Celebs and others . . .

Dan Quayle
Former Vice-president of the United States

Zesty Lemon Tea Bread

1/2 pound unsalted butter
3 cups sugar, divided
4 eggs
3 cups flour
1/2 teaspoon salt
2 teaspoons baking powder
2 1/2 tablespoons grated lemon rind
1/2 cup milk
1/2 cup half-and-half
juice of 3 lemons

In large bowl, cream butter and 2 cups sugar. Add eggs, one at a time, beating after each addition. Sift together flour, salt and baking powder. Combine with rind. Add to butter mixture alternating with combined milk and half and half. Mix well.

Pour into 2 greased 9 x 5- or 8 x 4-inch bread pans. Bake at 350° for 50 minutes or until tester comes out clean. While bread is baking, combine 1 cup sugar and lemon juice. Mix until sugar is dissolved. Pierce top of hot baked bread with fork in 10 or 20 places. Loosen sides from pan. Spoon juice mixture over top and sides.

Cool in pan 30 minutes. Remove from pan and finish cooling on rack.

DAN QUAYLE—*JD '74*
Former Vice-President of the United States
Indianapolis, Indiana

Chicken Enchiladas

12 corn tortillas
1/2 chopped green pepper
1 chopped medium sized onion
4 cups cooked chicken
1 pound grated cheese
1 small can evaporated milk
1 small can green chilies, chopped
2 cans cream of chicken soup
1 8-ounce carton sour cream

Combine soup, green pepper, chilies, onion, milk. Heat until bubbly. Turn off heat, stir in sour cream. Put small amount of sauce in bottom of a deep 9 x 13-inch pan. Line dish with half of tortillas. Lay half of chicken (shredded) over tortillas, half of sauce and half of cheese. Repeat, ending with cheese.

Bake covered for 30 minutes at 350°. Let stand 20 minutes before serving.

RANDALL TOBIAS—*BS '64*
CEO–Chairman Eli Lilly Co.
Indianapolis, Indiana

Evan Bayh
Governor of Indiana

Governor and Mrs. Bayh's Favorite Bar-B-Que

Sauce:

2 large cans tomato sauce
1 large Frank's hot sauce
4 tablespoons crushed red pepper
1 box brown sugar
4 tablespoons onion powder
4 tablespoons garlic powder
1 small bottle white vinegar
3 tablespoons vanilla

Stir ingredients well and then let it sit.

This keeps in the refrigerator for up to two months, and will get stronger the longer it sits.

EVAN BAYH—*BS '78*
Governor, State of Indiana
Indianapolis, Indiana

"Here are three recipes I make often. A good cold night and a hot basketball game, and you can sit down with friends and enjoy a good meal and an exciting game."

— W.M.

Beef Borscht

1 pound lean beef chuck, trimmed of fat and cut in 3/4-inch cubes
1 or 2 bay leaves
2 tablespoons cooking oil
3 cups coarsely chopped cabbage
2 cups peeled and cubed potatoes
1/2 cup chopped onions
1/4 cup chopped green peppers
1 tablespoon dried parsley flakes
1 14 1/2-ounce can of beef broth
1/2 teaspoon dried dillweed
1 16-ounce can tomatoes, cut up
1/4 cup half-and-half cream

1. In a large kettle, brown the meat in oil. Add 3 cups water and bay leaves. Bring to boil. Reduce heat, cover and simmer for 50 to 60 minutes or till the meat is nearly tender.

2. Stir in cabbage, potatoes, onions, green pepper, parsley flakes, beef broth and dill weed. Bringing to a boil. Reduce heat. Cover and simmer 25 to 30 minutes more or till meat and potatoes are tender. Stir in tomatoes; heat through, remove from heat.

3. Season with salt and pepper. Stir in cream and remove bay leaves. Serve six.

WILLIAM MOBERLY—*BS '83*
Retired, Chrysler Corporation Management
Kokomo, Indiana

Herb Rolls

3 to 3 1/2 cups all purpose flour
1 package active dry yeast
1 cup milk
1/4 cup sugar
1/4 cup margarine
1 clove garlic, minced
1/2 teaspoon salt
1 egg
4 ounces shredded provolone cheese
1 tablespoon chopped parsley
3 ounces grated parmesan cheese
2 teaspoons chopped chives

1. In a large mixer bowl, combinc 1 1/2 cups flour and the yeast.

2. In saucepan, combine milk, sugar, butter, garlic and 1/2 teaspoon salt. Heat and stir till just warm and butter almost melts.

3. Add this mixture to flour along with egg. Beat with electric mixer on low speed for 30 seconds, scraping the mixer bowl constantly. Beat on high speed for 3 minutes.

4. Stir in cheese, parsley and chives. Stir in as much of the remaining flour as you can with a spoon.

5. Turn dough out on to a lightly floured surface. Knead in enough remaining flour to make a moderately stiff dough that is smooth and elastic (6 to 8 minutes). Shape dough in ball and place in a lightly greased bowl. Turn once to grease the surface. Cover and let rise in a warm place till doubled (about 1 hour).

6. Punch down dough. Turn out onto a lightly floured surface. Divide dough in half, cover; let rest 10 minutes.

7. Divide each portion into 12 pieces; shape into rolls, place on lightly greased baking sheet. Cover, let rise in warm place till nearly doubled (30 minutes).

8. Bake in a 325° oven for about 20 minutes or till golden brown. Makes 24 rolls.

WILLIAM MOBERLY—*BS '83*
Retired, Chrysler Corporation Management
Kokomo, Indiana

Three Layer Carrot Cake

2 cups all-purpose flour
2 cups sugar
1 tablespoon ground cinnamon
2 teaspoons baking soda
1 teaspoon salt
dash of ground allspice
4 eggs
1 cup cooking oil
4 cups finely shredded carrots (about 1 to 1 1/3 pounds)
1/2 cup apricot preserves

1. Grease and flour three 8 1/2 x 1 1/2-inch round baking pans and set aside.

2. In a bowl, stir together the flour, sugar, cinnamon, baking soda, salt and allspice.

3. In a mixer bowl, beat eggs with an electric mixer till light and frothy. Beat on medium speed while adding oil. At low speed, beat in flour mixture just till batter is smooth.

4. By hand, stir in carrots. Pour into prepared pans. Bake in a 350° oven for 20-25 minutes or until done. Cool on wire racks 10 minutes. Remove from pans and cool.

5. Prepare cream cheese frosting (recipe follows).

Cream Cheese Frosting

In a large bowl, beat until light and fluffy
1 softened 8 ounce package cream cheese
1/3 cup softened unsalted butter
1/2 teaspoon vanilla

Gradually beat in enough powdered sugar (about 3 cups) to make spreadable frosting.

To assemble, set one cake layer on a serving plate. Spread apricot preserves over the cake top. Top with second layer and spread apricot preserves on this layer. Place third layer on top. Spread sides and top of cake with cream cheese frosting. Sprinkle 1/4 cup chopped nuts on top. Store covered in refrigerator.

WILLIAM MOBERLY—*BS '83*
Retired, Chrysler Corp. Management
Kokomo. Indiana

United States Senator Dan Coats

Senator Dan Coats' mother was born in Sweden and this is a family recipe. Vera Swanlund Coats passed this recipe on to Marcia Coats. Swedish meat balls is a Coats family traditional Christmas dish.

Swedish Meat Balls

3/4 pound ground beef
1/2 pound ground veal
1/4 pound ground pork
1 1/2 cups soft bread crumbs
1 cup light cream
1/2 cup chopped onion
1 egg
1/4 cup finely chopped parsley
1 1/2 teaspoons salt
1/4 teaspoon ginger
1/8 teaspoon pepper
1/8 teaspoon nutmeg

Gravy
2 tablespoons all purpose flour
1 cup light cream
1/2 teaspoon instant coffee

Have meat ground together twice. Soak bread in cream for 5 minutes. Cook onion in 1 tablespoon butter till tender. Mix meats, crumb mixture, onion, egg, parsley and seasonings. Beat vigorously till fluffy (5 minutes on medium speed or 8 minutes by hand). Form into 1 1/2-inch balls (easier to do with wet hands and chilled mixture). Brown lightly in 2 tablespoons butter, shaking skillet to keep balls round (don't try to do too many at once). Remove balls. Reserve drippings.

To make gravy, stir flour into drippings in skillet, add light cream and coffee. Heat and stir till gravy thickens. Return balls to gravy, cover, cook slowly about 30 minutes, basting occasionally. Makes 3 dozen.

DAN COATS—*JD '72*
United States Senator
Washington, DC

Wassail

4 cups pineapple juice
4 cups cider
1 cup orange juice
1 1/2 cups apricot nectar
1 6-inch cinnamon stick
1 teaspoon whole cloves

Combine all ingredients. Bring to a boil and simmer 20 minutes

Strain before serving. Makes 9 cups.

DAN COATS—*JD '72*
United States Senator
Washington, DC

Pork Tenderloin "Towers"

3/4 pound pork tenderloin (cut in about 4 to 6 pieces)
sliced onion
sliced tomato
Velveeta slices
bacon strips
toothpicks

1. Pound pork pieces thin
2. Salt & pepper them
3. Place slice of onion, slice of tomato, slice of Velveeta and slice of bacon (cut in 2 pieces) on top of each tenderloin piece.
4. Put toothpicks in each tower.

Bake 1 hour at 350°

BOB BRAASCH—*BA '89*
Sales Manager
Evanston, Illinois

Mary's Taco Platter

1 large avocado
8 ounces cream cheese
1 teaspoon lemon juice
2 tablespoons mayonnaise
4 ounces sour cream
salt and pepper

Puree the ingredients in food processor or blender. Spread on platter. Top with 8-10 green onions, 5 chopped tomatoes, 8-10 ounces shredded cheddar cheese. Sprinkle with chili powder and serve with taco chips.

LAURA WOOD HOGG—*BS '85*
Homemaker
Mishawaka, Indiana

Rouladen

1 slice round steak, 1/4 inch thick
bacon
onion
salt
mustard
flour
pepper

Trim out bone of round steak and trim off all fat. Cut meat along veins. A few will be large—cut these in half.

Spread each piece with mustard, then strip of bacon and some chopped onion.

Roll into bundles and secure with tooth picks. Dredge in flour and brown in fat. A good brown crust adds to flavor.

When well browned, add water and cover. Simmer or bake for 1 1/2 to 2 hours, adding more water if necessary.

OTIS BOWEN, MD—*'42, LLD '76*
Retired, former Governor of Indiana
Bremen, Indiana

Joseph Hogsett
Indiana Secretary of State

Sugar Cream Pie

1 cup sugar
5 teaspoons flour
1 1/2 cups unwhipped whipping cream
1 9-inch unbaked pie shell
1/4 stick margarine

Blend flour and sugar with whisk. Slowly pour in whipping cream and blend until smooth. Pour into unbaked pie shell. Dot with margarine.

Bake at 370° for 10 minutes then at 350° for 25 to 30 minutes.

Sprinkle top with cinnamon if desired.

JOSEPH HOGSETT—*JD '81*
Secretary of State, Indiana
Indianapolis, Indiana

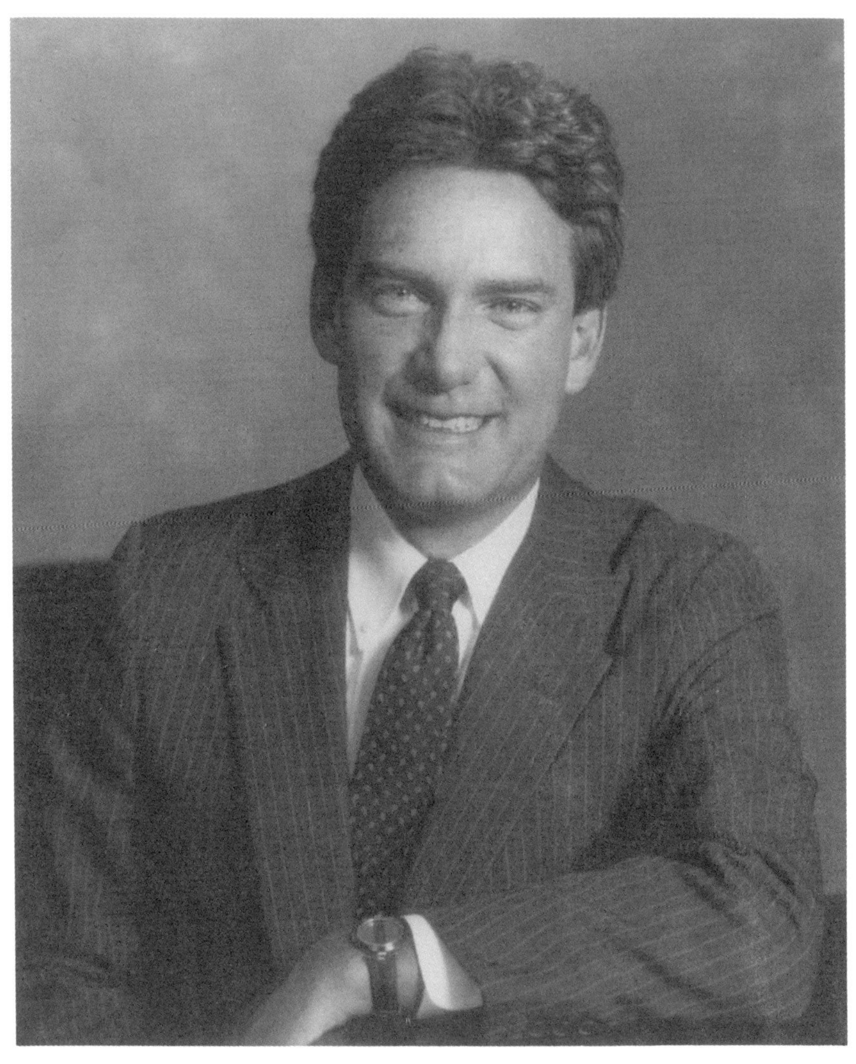

Paul Helmke
Mayor of Fort Wayne, Indiana

Spanakopeeta

1 package frozen chopped spinach
3 beaten eggs
6 tablespoons flour
2 cups cottage cheese
2 cups grated cheddar cheese
1/2 teaspoon salt

Thaw frozen chopped spinach. Squeeze out as much water as possible. Spinach should be dry.

Beat eggs and flour until smooth. Add rest of ingredients. Mix well. Bake uncovered in a 2-quart casserole, 350° for 60 minutes.

Watch closely so casserole does not become too dry.

Let stand 1-2 minutes before cutting into squares. Serves 6.

PAUL HELMKE—*BA '70*
Mayor, City of Fort Wayne
Fort Wayne, Indiana

Green Chili Quiche

2 medium zucchini, shredded (squeeze out excess water)
2 finely chopped green onions
1/4 cup chopped green chiles, canned
4 beaten egg whites
2 eggs or egg substitute
1 cup grated part skim mozzarella
1 cup grated cheddar cheese
1 1/2 cups evaporated skim milk
vegetable coating spray

Saute squash and onion in a nonstick skillet over low heat until tender. Add water if squash begins to stick.

Mix all ingredients and pour into 9-inch pan sprayed with vegetable coating spray.

Bake at 350° until firm and lightly browned. You may put into a pie crust if you wish. Serves 8.

JANIE FRICKE—*BS '72*
Country-Western Singer
Lancaster, Texas

Texana Layered Mexican Dip

2 16-ounce cans refried beans (warm)
1/2 pound cooked hamburger meat (warm)
1 1/2 cups grated cheese
2 6-ounce containers avocado dip
1 8-ounce carton sour cream

Spread the first five ingredients on a large platter in even layers in order listed.

If desired garnish with jalepeño peppers or pico de gallo and serve with warm chips.

Makes approximately 12 servings.

JANIE FRICKE—*BS '72*
Country-Western Singer
Lancaster, Texas

Frank O'Bannon
Indiana Lieutenant Governor

"This recipe is one my grandmother always made and is a tradition in our family."

— F.O'B.

Carmels

4 cups granulated sugar
2 cups light corn syrup
6 cups light cream
1/8 teaspoon salt

Mix corn syrup and sugar with 2 cups cream; heat to soft ball stage.

Add 2 cups of cream slowly and continue to cook to soft ball stage.

Add last 2 cups of cream and cook to hard ball stage pour immediately on to a greased cookie pan.

One end of pan can be covered with walnuts which will help loosen carmels from pan. When cool, cut into squares.

FRANK O'BANNON—*JD '57*
Lieutenant Governor, State of Indiana
Indianapolis, Indiana

Marilyn Tucker Quayle
Author and attorney

Brownies with Fresh Raspberry Sauce

1 pint fresh raspberries
1 or 2 tablespoons superfine sugar
2 teaspoons lemon juice
4 brownies
creme fraîche or whipped cream

Puree all but 1/2 cup berries in food processor or blender until smooth. Press through fine sieve to remove seeds, if desired. Add sugar and lemon juice; stir until sugar dissolves.

Divide sauce equally among 4 dessert plates. Top with brownie and garnish with creme fraîche or whipped cream and remaining berries.

Serves 4.

MARILYN TUCKER QUAYLE—***JD '74***
Author, attorney
Indianapolis, Indiana

Carrot Salad

3 cups grated carrots
1 cup seedless raisins
6 tablespoons mayonnaise
1/4 cup milk
1 tablespoon lime juice (optional)
1/2 cup shredded coconut
pinch salt

Toss carrots and raisins together. Blend remaining ingredients and pour over mixture. Stir carefully and thoroughly. Chill overnight (if convenient) to blend flavors.

"I can remember the beautiful aroma coming from my mother's kitchen on fall afternoons when she made this tasty recipe."

—W.T.J.

Apple Butter

2 dozen medium apples quartered (any variety)
2 quarts apple cider or water

Cook together until tender. Press through sieve or food mill

Add to above:
3 cups sugar

1 1/2 teaspoons ground cinnamon
1 teaspoon ground cloves

Bake in dutch oven at 325° all afternoon, stirring occasionally. May be canned, frozen, or stored in refrigerator for approximately three weeks.

WILLIAM T. JACKLIN—*MS '68*
DuPage County Auditor
Wheaton, Illinois

Lemon Meringue Pie

1 can Eagle Brand Condensed milk
1/2 cup fresh lemon juice
1 teaspoon grated lemon peel
3 egg yolks, well beaten

Combine above ingredients

Beat 3 egg whites until stiff, and fold in 6 tablespoons white sugar.

Put lemon mixture in baked pie shell and add egg whites.

Bake at 325° for 20 minutes.

Harold Poling—*MBA '51*
CEO, Ford Motor Company
Dearborn, Michigan

H. Dean Evans
Former Indiana State Superintendant of Public Instruction

Special K Brownies

3/4 cup white corn syrup
3/4 cup light brown sugar

Bring to boil in a large pan and remove from burner.

Add:
1 cup crunchy peanut butter and
5 cups Special K cereal

Stir until well coated. Press into 9 x 13-inch buttered pan.

Topping

Over low heat melt:
1 6-ounce package butterscotch bits
1 6-ounce package chocolate chips

Spread on top and let set. You may refrigerate to set topping. Cut into squares.

H. DEAN EVANS—*EDD '66*
Former Indiana State Superintendent of Public Instruction
Indianapolis, Indiana

"Penuchi bars are favorites of my children, both IU graduates, Jim Jontz and Mary Lee Jontz Turk, and of my grandchildren who will someday, I hope, also be IU grads."

—P.J.

Penuchi Bars

1/2 cup butter
1/2 cup light brown sugar
1 cup flour
1/2 teaspoon salt
1/2 teaspoon baking powder

Mix and bake 15 minutes in greased 9 x 9-inch pan, 350°.

Mix and pour over above mixture:
2 eggs
1 cup light brown sugar
2 tablespoon flour
1/2 teaspoon baking powder
1/4 teaspoon salt
1 1/2 cups nuts
1 teaspoon vanilla

Bake another 25 minutes at 350°. Cool, cut into squares.

POLLY JONTZ—*AB '49*
President, Conner Prairie
Fishers, Indiana

"I...learned (this recipe) as a kid listening to the TV commercial jingle for 'Fluffer-Nutters.' I remember those sandwiches with 100 percent of the minimum daily requirements of glucose, sucrose, and dextrose. The lyrics I sang along with were..."

— M.U.

"Fluffer-Nutters"

"Oh, you need Fluff, Fluff, Fluff,
To make a Fluffer-Nutter.
Marshmallow Fluff,
And lots of Peanut Butter.
First you spread, spread, spread,
Your bread with Peanut Butter,
Add Marshmallow Fluff
To have a Fluffer-Nutter.
Oh, you'll enjoy, joy, joy,
Your bread with peanut butter.
You'll be glad to have enough,
For another Fluffer-Nutter."

MICHAEL USLAN—*JD '76*
Executive Producer, "Batman"
Cedar Grove, New Jersey

Jill Long
United States House of Representatives

Favorite Raspberry Pie

Pastry:

1/3 cup butter
2 1/2 tablespoons sugar
1/3 teaspoon salt
1 egg yolk
1 cup flour
1/3 cup finely chopped almonds

Filling:

1 10-ounce package frozen raspberries, thawed and drained
2 egg whites
1 cup sugar
1 tablespoon lemon juice
1/4 teaspoon vanilla
1/4 teaspoon almond extract
1/8 teaspoon salt
1 cup whipping cream

Preheat oven to 400°. Grease a 9-inch pie pan. Cream butter, sugar and salt until fluffy. Add egg yolk and beat thoroughly. Mix in flour and almonds.

Press into prepared pie pan. Bake 12 minutes; cool.

Place all ingredients for filling except whipping cream in large bowl. Beat until it thickens, approximately 15 minutes. Whip cream and fold into raspberry mixture. Pile into pastry and freeze at least 8 hours.

JILL LONG—*PhD '84*
United States House of Representatives
Washington, DC

Lee Hamilton
United States House of Representatives

Strawberry Pie

1 quart fresh strawberries
1/2 cup sugar (suit to taste)
1 tablespoon cornstarch
1 baked pie shell

Mash 1/3 of berries; mix with cornstarch and sugar. Cook 10 minutes on low heat, stirring constantly. Cool. Add remaining uncrushed berries; stir to coat berries.

Put in baked pie shell and chill.

Serve with whipped cream. Serves 6.

LEE HAMILTON—*JD '56*
United States House of Representatives
Washington, DC

Sandbakkelse

1/2 cup butter
2 teaspoons vanilla or almond extract
1/2 cup margarine
1/2 teaspoon salt
1 cup sugar
2 3/4 cups flour
2 eggs

Cream the butter, gradually add sugar. Add eggs, beat well and add vanilla extract. Add flour. Chill dough.

Press dough firmly into lightly floured sandbakkelse tins, making a thin hollow shell, cutting it off around the top edge. Place tins on cookie sheet.

Bake in moderate oven 10 minutes or until a light brown. When done remove tins and place on a board upside down to partially cool. (NOTE: I tap tins with knife to help cookie fall out.)

LEE HAMILTON—*JD '56*
United States House of Representatives
Washington, DC

Dog Biscuits

1 cup flour
1 cup wheat flour
1/2 cup wheat germ
1/2 cup powdered milk (or soy milk)
1/2 teaspoon salt
6 tablespoons oleo (or hard bacon fat)
1 teaspoon brown sugar
1 egg
water

Combine flour, milk and salt in bowl, cut in oleo until mix resembles corn meal. Stir sugar with egg and add to dry ingredients. Add 1/2 cup water to make a stiff dough.

Knead dough on floured board until smooth, roll 1/2 inch thick and cut with cookie cutter.

Bake 20 minutes at 350° on a greased cookie sheet.

LEE HAMILTON—*JD '56*
United States House of Representatives
Washington, DC

Sports heroes
and others . . .

Bob Knight
Head coach, IU men's basketball

Coconut Cake

1 package yellow or white cake mix, with pudding in the mix
1/4 cup oil
1 1/2 cups water
2 cups coconut
2 eggs
1 can cream of coconut
1 medium size tub of whipped topping

Mix the cake mix, oil, eggs, water, 1 cup cream of coconut and 1 cup coconut. Bake 350° for 35 minutes in 9 x 13-inch pan. Punch holes in cake and pour rest of cream of coconut over cake, let cool and frost with 1 cup coconut and whipped topping.

Refrigerate.

BOB KNIGHT
Head Coach, Men's Basketball
Bloomington, Indiana

Hash Brown Casserole

2 pounds frozen hash browns
1 teaspoon salt
1 can cream of chicken soup
pepper
1 pint sour cream
10 ounces shredded cheddar cheese
1/4 cup chopped onion

Completely thaw hash browns. Mix together the next five ingredients. Put into a 9 x 13-inch pan. Sprinkle cheese on top. Dot with 1/4 cup butter before baking.

Bake at 350° for 45 minutes.

TRACY E. LITTLE—*JD '66*
Senior Vice-President
Northern Capital Management
Thiensville, Wisconsin

Oranges and Kiwi Curacao

8 navel oranges
4 kiwi fruit
boiling water
2/3 cup water
2/3 cup sugar
1/3 cup curacao (or other flavor liqueur)

1. Peel 6 oranges, cut in crosswise cartwheel slices. Place in bowl.

2. Peel kiwis, slice crosswise into 1/4-inch thick slices, add to oranges.

3. Peel remaining 2 oranges thinly, removing outer colored peel only. Cut peel into thin slivers.

4. Squeeze juice from peeled oranges, reserve.

5. In small saucepan, cover slivered peel with boiling water. Boil peel for five minutes, drain. This is called blanching.

6. Combine drained peel, 2/3 cup water, 2/3 cup sugar and reserved orange juice; heat, stirring, just until sugar dissolves. Add curacao, pour over oranges and kiwi.

7. Cover bowl and chill four hours or longer. If making the day before, add kiwi slices on day serving as they are very delicate tender fruit.

JAMES "DOC" COUNSILMAN
Retired Swimming Coach
Bloomington, Indiana

"Great served with sharp cheddar cheese, crackers and any IU sport on TV."

—M.C.W.

Barbecue Meatballs (appetizer)

Meatballs:

2 pounds lean ground beef
1 1/2 cups Italian-style bread crumbs
1/2 cup finely chopped onion
1 cup milk
1 egg
1/4 teaspoon each salt and pepper
1/4 teaspoon ginger
1/4 teaspoon nutmeg

Whisk together milk, egg and spices. Mix in ground beef, bread crumbs and onion. Mix together thoroughly and shape into 1-inch balls. Bake uncovered in 350° oven for 25-30 minutes, until cooked through. Drain on paper towels.

Sauce:

1 cup barbecue sauce (spicy or mild)
1 cup ketchup
1/2 cup brown sugar
2 tablespoons vinegar
2 tablespoons Worcestershire sauce
1/4 teaspoon each of salt and pepper
1/2 cup water

Mix all ingredients together and cook slowly until thick (20-35 minutes). Add meatballs and stir carefully. Simmer 15-30 minutes, stirring occasionally.

M. CHILDS-WATSON—*BS '72, MS '75*
Human Resource Manager
Chrysler Corporation
Farmington Hills, Michigan

Wild Rice Casserole

Combine in casserole:
1 box Uncle Ben's Wild Rice with seasoning
1/8 pound butter (1/2 stick), melted
4 tablespoons chopped onion
1 small can mushrooms
1/2 teaspoon salt
1 can water chestnuts sliced
1 16-ounce can chicken broth
1 can cream of chicken soup

Cover and refrigerate for at least 24 hours. Bring to room temperature. Bake at 325° for 1 1/2 hours.

NANCY L. WAIT—*BS '77*
Co-owner, Frederick Tool Corp.
Elkhart, Indiana

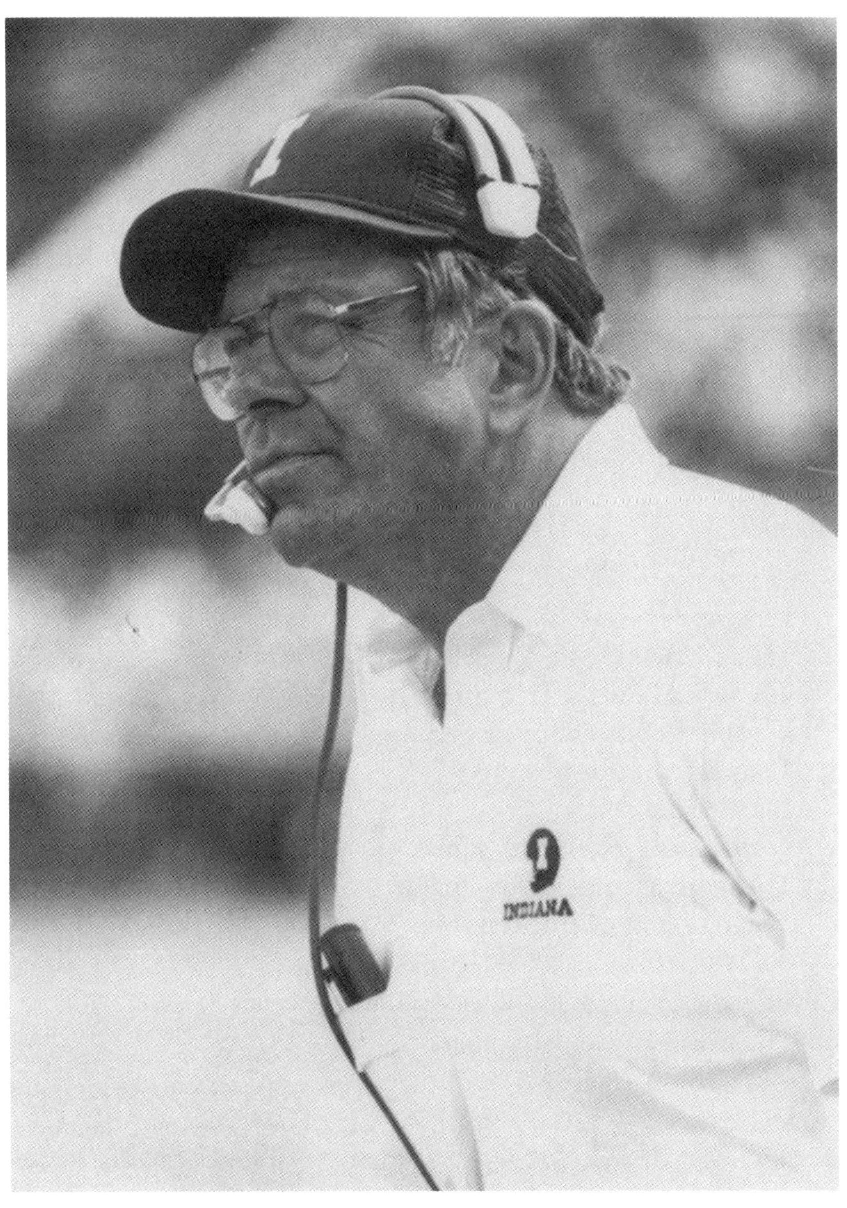

Bill Mallory
Head coach, IU men's football

Easy Graham Cracker Pudding Dish

cooked vanilla pudding
graham crackers
whipped cream
chopped nuts

Make pudding. Lay one layer of whole graham crackers in an 8 x 8-inch dish.

Cover with 1/3 hot pudding.

Cover with second layer of crackers and second layer of pudding.

Continue with third layer of each.

Cool. Spread with whipped cream and sprinkle with nuts.

WILLIAM MALLORY
Head Coach, Men's Football
Bloomington, Indiana

Chocolate Silk

Graham Cracker Crust:
18 squares of graham crackers crushed
1/3 cup sugar
1/2 cup margarine or butter, melted

Mix together and press in cake pan (9 x 13 inches).

Filling:
1 cup butter or margarine, softened
1 1/2 cups sugar
4 ounces unsweetened chocolate, melted
4 eggs

Cream sugar and butter. Beat in melted chocolate, add eggs, one at a time, beating after each addition. Spoon lightly into crust. Garnish with shaved chocolate curls. Refrigerate.

NANCY L. WAIT—*BS '77*
Co-owner, Frederick Tool Corp.
Elkhart, Indiana

Burrito Bake

1 cup buttermilk baking mix
1/4 cup water
1 16-ounce can refried beans
1 pound ground beef browned and drained
1 cup thick salsa
1 1/2 cups shredded cheese
sour cream, lettuce, tomato

Grease 10 x 1 1/2-inch pie plate. Combine baking mix, water and beans. Spread on plate. Layer ground beef, salsa, and shredded cheese on bean mixture. Bake in a 375° oven for 30 minutes. Serve with sour cream, lettuce and tomato.

NANCY L. WAIT—*BS '77*
Co-owner, Frederick Tool Corp.
Elkhart, Indiana

French Baked Pancake

1/2 cup margarine
4 teaspoons sugar
3 large eggs
2 cups flour
1 1/2 teaspoons baking powder
2/3 cup milk

In a mixing bowl, cream margarine and sugar. Beat in eggs. In another bowl, combine flour and baking powder. Add alternately with milk to margarine/egg mixture; Mix well. Pour half of batter into a well greased 13 x 9 baking dish.

Prepare Filling:
24 ounces small curd cottage cheese
3 tablespoons melted butter
1 teaspoon salt
2 eggs

Combine all and spread over batter in baking dish. Top with remaining batter.

Bake at 350° for 45 minutes or until golden brown. Cut in 3-inch square pieces and serve hot with toppings such as syrup, yogurt, honey, fruit preserves, or sour cream. Makes 6-8 servings, 1-2 pieces each.

NANCY L. WAIT—*BS '77*
Co-owner, Frederick Tool Corp.
Elkhart, Indiana

"This was my mother's recipe and was quickly known as 'Marie's Macaroni' and requested at reunions, family and church gatherings. You'll love it."

—S.R.

Marie's Macaroni and Cheese

1 7-ounce box of macaroni
1 1/2 pounds of block yellow American cheese
1 egg
2 cups whole milk
1-plus tablespoon butter
paprika, salt and pepper

Bring 2 quarts of water to a boil (do NOT add salt to the water) add macaroni, return to boil; cook 7 minutes, uncovered and stirring frequently. Drain, rinse with cold water and drain again. Place approximately half of the macaroni into a 2-quart glass baking dish. Cover with American cheese cut into 1/4-inch cubes sprinkle with salt and pepper. Add second half of macaroni and salt and pepper the second half. Cover thickly with remaining cheese cubes (3 good fistfuls). Beat one egg in bowl, and add 2 cups milk. Pour over macaroni—milk should start to come up the side of dish. Sprinkle with paprika. Slice 1 tablespoon butter over top.

Bake at 350° for 45 minutes to 1 hour uncovered.

SUSAN RASMUSSEN—*MS '73*
Research Nurse, Krannert Institute Cardiology
Indianapolis, Indiana

Big Red works its way toward a touchdown.

Kahlua Fudge Brownies

1 1/2 cups sifted flour
1/2 teaspoon baking powder
1/2 teaspoon salt
3 large eggs
2 cups sugar
1/4 cup Kahlua
2/3 cup butter
3 1-ounce squares unsweetened chocolate
3/4 cup chopped walnuts
1 tablespoon Kahlua & powdered sugar for tops of bars

Resift flour with baking powder and salt. Melt butter with chocolate over very low heat in burn-proof pan. Beat eggs with sugar until light. Stir in chocolate mixture and mix well with 1/4 cup Kahlua. Add flour mixture and mix well. Stir in walnuts. Pour into greased 9-inch square pan. Bake in center of oven at 350° for 30–40 minutes until top springs back when touched and edges pull away from pan. Don't over bake—brownies will be gooey. Cool in pan; brush with 1 tablespoon Kahlua. Sprinkle with sifted powdered sugar. Wrap in foil to keep fresh.

THOMAS SHOJI
Head Coach, Women's Volleyball
Bloomington, Indiana

Virginia's Party Meatballs

Meatballs:
1 1/2 pounds lean beef round, ground
1 cup bread crumbs
1 can diced water chestnuts
1 egg
1/2 cup water
2 1/2 tablespoons horseradish

Sauce:
1 11-ounce can mandarin oranges
1/2 cup orange marmalade
1/2 cup water
2 tablespoons lemon juice
1/4 cup soy sauce
dash of garlic salt

Combine all ingredients. Form into 1 1/4-inch balls. Arrange single layers of balls in shallow pan.Bake 1/2 hour 350° oven. Drain.

Combine orange marmalade, water, lemon juice, soy sauce and garlic salt in saucepan. Bring to a boil. Remove from heat. Gently stir in mandarin orange segments.

Place meatballs in a chafing dish. Pour sauce over meatballs. Serve in chafing dish with toothpicks. Yield: 42 meatballs.

VIRGINIA LEE COWAN SIMMONS—*Ed S '70*
Former Elementary Principal
Boca Raton, Florida

Pineapple Upside Down Cake

2/3 cup margarine
2 20-ounce cans crushed pineapple (packed in juice)
1 cup brown sugar
1 18.25-ounce package 3-egg yellow cake mix

Whipped cream and maraschino cherries

1. Preheat oven to 350°
2. As oven preheats, melt margarine in 9 x 13-inch baking dish in oven.
3. Sprinklc brown sugar evenly over margarine.
4. Drain pineapple and arrange on butter/sugar mixture.
5. Prepare 3-egg cake batter according to package directions; Pour over fruit.
6. Bake 35 to 45 minutes.
7. Cake is done when top springs back when lightly touched.
8. Remove from oven, let cool 5 minutes.
9. Turn onto serving plate with pineapple side up. Sugar mixture will soak in and run down over cake.

Serve warm with whipped cream and maraschino cherries. Serves sixteen.

MIRIAM STEMLE BOYD—*MO '62*
Optometrist
Vincennes, Indiana

IU's defense blocks Michigan.

Steve Alford
Basketball coach, Manchester College, New Castle, Indiana

Five-Layer Extravaganza

2 packages Cinnamon Crisps
5 tablespoons melted butter
2 cups powdered sugar
2 eggs
1 stick butter or margarine
3 bananas, sliced lengthwise
1 No. 2 can crushed pineapple, drained
2 packages whipped topping mix
crushed pecans
12 maraschino cherries

Crush crisps, add melted butter. Press into 2-quart dish. Mix together powdered sugar, eggs and 1 stick butter, spread over crust. Put bananas on top. Sprinkle pineapple over bananas. Prepare whipped topping, spread over pineapple. Sprinkle with pecans and arrange cherries on top. Refrigerate overnight.

STEPHEN T. ALFORD—*BS '87*
Basketball Coach, Manchester College
New Castle, Indiana

Blueberry Muffins

2 cups all purpose flour
3 teaspoons baking powder
1/2 teaspoon salt
1/4 cup sugar
1 egg well beaten
1 cup milk
6 tablespoons or 1/3 cup oil

Sift together flour, baking powder, salt and 1/4 cup sugar. Combine the egg, milk and oil and add all at once to the flour mixture. Stir until dry ingredients are moist, but still lumpy. Fold in 1/2 cup blueberries.

Fill greased muffin pans 2/3 full. Sprinkle with 1 tablespoon sugar. Bake at 400° about 25 minutes

Blueberries can be fresh or frozen—you can use up to 3/4 cup if you really like them!

PHOEBE ANN BUEL BOZE—*GN '53*
Retired nurse, volunteer, clown
Berne, Indiana

Busy Day Stew

1 1/2 pounds beef, cubed
1 16-ounce can stewed tomatoes
6 carrots
1 cup celery chunks
4 potatoes
3 medium onions sliced
1 teaspoon salt
1 tablespoon sugar
1/4 cup tapioca (quick cooking type)

Clean and dice all vegetables into large chunks. Mix all ingredients in a large casserole dish or Dutch oven. Bake covered at 250° for 5 hours.

(NOTE: Do not prebrown the meat. The stew makes its own gravy.)

GLEN A. HICKS—*BS '66*
High school teacher
Ligonier, Indiana

Garlic Spinach Lasagna

16 ounces frozen spinach
10 ounces lasagna noodles (about 10 noodles)
3 cups cream-style cottage cheese (about 1 1/2 pounds, small curd)
1 clove garlic
1 tablespoon parsley flakes
2 eggs, well beaten
1 tablespoon basil
1 teaspoon salt
1 teaspoon pepper
1 1-pound can tomatoes and juice
2 tablespoons parsley flakes
12 ounces tomato sauce
1/2 cup parmesan cheese, grated
3 tablespoons garlic powder
1 pound mozzarella cheese, sliced thin

Boil spinach according to instructions. Drain well. Place spinach in skillet with next 7 ingredients. Simmer uncovered until sauce is thick, about 12-15 minutes, stirring occasionally.

Cook noodles in boiling salted water according to instructions, then leave in cold water. Combine cottage cheese, eggs, other seasonings and parmesan cheese. Place half the cooked noodles in 9 x 13 x 2-inch baking dish. Spread half the cottage cheese mix over noodles; add half mozzarella cheese layer, and half spinach paste sauce. Repeat layers. Bake, covered with aluminum foil, for 30 minutes; uncover and continue baking for 10 more minutes. Let stand 10–15 minutes before serving.

Serves 8–10 persons. After one serving, garlic can be increased for heartier appetites!

STEVEN J. RIGGS—*JD '86*
Trial attorney
San Diego, California

Cauliflower Marinade

1 head cauliflower
1 small jar stuffed olives
red onion rings to taste
1 4-ounce package crumbled blue cheese
1 cup oil and vinegar, mixed 3 to 1

Cut cauliflower in small pieces, slice olives, add onion rings and blue cheese. Pour vinegar and oil over all, mix and marinate all day. Mix several times during day.

Serves 4 or 5 as salad.

JEROME WILLIAM OSTERTAG—*BS '50*
Owner, Zipper Air Conditioning
Louisville, Kentucky

Bill's Beefy Beans

2 cans pork and beans (16 ounces each)
1 can kidney beans (16 ounces)
1 1/2 to 2 pound hamburger (browned and drained)
1 package dry onion soup mix
1 cup ketchup
1 cup water
1 tablespoon mustard
2 teaspoons vinegar

Brown and drain hamburger. Mix all ingredients in large baking dish. Bake uncovered for 1 hour at 400°.

Excellent for picnics!

BILL HAMMACK—*JD '74*
District Counsel, IRS
Plano, Texas

Sportscaster Dick Enberg

Lemon Squares

2 cups flour
1/2 cup confectioner's sugar
1 cup butter or margarine
1 lemon rind (grated)
1/2 cup lemon juice
4 eggs, beaten
3/4 cup sugar
1/4 cup flour
1 teaspoon baking powder

Icing

1 cup confectioner's sugar
1 to 2 tablespoons lemon juice

Mix together the flour and the 1/2 cup confectioner's sugar. Cut in the butter with a pastry blender until it resembles cornmeal. Pack into a lightly greased 13 x 9-inch pan. Bake 15 minutes at 350°. Cool.

Grate the rind of the lemon and mix with the lemon juice. Mix the eggs, sugar, flour and baking powder. Pour into the cooled crust and bake 25-30 minutes at 350°. Cool slightly and frost with icing of sugar and lemon juice.

DICK ENBERG, Doctor of Health and Safety—'62
NBC Sportscaster
Rancho Santa Fe, California

This recipe is "excellent for 'special dinners,' as well as picnics!"

— J.S.H.

Casserole That Men Love

(aka—Cheesy Potatoes)

1 32-ounce package frozen hash brown potatoes, partially thawed
1 cup sour cream
onion salt
2 cans cream of potato soup
8 ounces or more shredded cheddar cheese
1 tablespoon parmesan cheese

Mix together all ingredients except parmesan cheese. Season with onion salt. Spread into greased 11 x 14-inch baking dish. Sprinkle with parmesan cheese. Bake, uncovered, 1 hour at 350°.

JAN SHUTT HAMMACK—*MS '78*
Mother
Plano, Texas

Working Woman's Barbecued Pork With Rice

7 or 8 lean, thin pork chops (cut off excess fat around edges)
1 standard bottle of a favorite barbecue sauce

In the morning before leaving for work:
Broil pork chops to burn off excess fat and to brown. Place pork chops in an electric crock pot and pour barbecue sauce over them. Place in crock pot on medium or low temperature to cook with the following:

1/4 cup olive oil
2 sweet green pepper, chopped
1 large Spanish onion, chopped
3 stalks celery, chopped
3 cloves garlic, minced (or powdered)

Saute vegetables in olive oil until slightly softened. Add to meat in crock pot. Allow mixture to cook all day.

Before supper: Prepare 6–8 servings of rice by substituting one 14-ounce can of diced tomatoes for 1 cup of water in rice package directions. (NOTE: I microwave the rice for the number of minutes—usually 25—suggested in the stove top cooking instructions.)

Stir meat mixture; meat should be falling off bone and be very tender. If your pork chops were not boneless, remove bones from crock pot mixture. Stir cooked rice into meat mixture and serve. Serves 6–8 people.

LILIAN CABAGE SWENSON—*MS '69*
Computer coordinator, journalism teacher
Dyer, Indiana

Crab au Gratin

4 tablespoons butter
4 tablespoons flour
2 cups milk or half-and-half
1 teaspoon salt
1/4 teaspoon pepper
1 1/2 tablespoons lemon juice
2 tablespoons grated onion
1 pound blue crab (lump or backfin)
grated cheddar cheese

Melt butter, blend in flour. Add milk or half-and-half stirring constantly until thickened. Add salt, pepper, lemon juice and grated onion. Remove from heat and fold in crab meat (make sure all shells and membranes have been removed). Put mixture into individual scallop shells or a casserole. Top with grated cheddar cheese.

Bake for 20-25 minutes at 375° or until bubbly. Serves 6–8.

HARRY B. LITTELL—*LLB '46*
Retired
Arlington, Virginia

Percolator Punch

1 quart apple cider or juice
1 pint cranberry juice cocktail
1 cup orange juice
3/4 cup lemon juice
1 cup sugar
1 teaspoon whole allspice
1 teaspoon whole cloves
3 sticks cinnamon

Combine the juices in a 20-cup percolator.

Place the sugar and spices in the percolator basket.

Plug in percolator and allow it to go through the "perk" cycle.

Serve hot.

Makes sixteen 1/2-cup servings.

CARRIE HICKS—*BA '85*
Systems analyst
Griffith, Indiana

"Coffee Grounds" Dessert

1 package chocolate sandwich cookies (crushed)
1/2 cup milk
2 eggs (separate yolks and whites)
2 dozen large marshmallows
6 chocolate bars with almonds (sliced into small pieces)
1 cup whipping cream, whipped

Butter a large deep baking dish. Put half of the crumbs in bottom. Put 1/4 cup milk in double boiler with marshmallows; heat until marshmallows start to melt. Add remaining milk and egg yolks; cook until like custard (careful not to overcook). Cool.

In separate bowl beat the 2 egg whites; mix with sliced chocolate bars. Fold in whipped cream.

Fold into custard mixture and pour on top of crumbs. Sprinkle top with remaining crumbs and chill.

KRISTINA KRIZMAN EDLEMAN—*BS '82*
Model
Savannah, Georgia

"Great for potlucks and cookouts. You might want to make more than one—it's always the first one gone!"

—K.K.E.

Five-Layer Chocolate Dessert

Layer 1 (crust)
3/4 cup finely chopped nuts
1 1/2 cups flour
1 stick margarine, softened

Mix and press into 9 x 13-inch pan and bake for 20 minutes at 350°. Cool.

Layer 2
Mix thoroughly
1 cup powdered sugar
1 8-ounce package cream cheese
fold in
1 cup frozen whipped topping, thawed
Spread over layer 1.

Layer 3
1 large package vanilla instant pudding
1 large package chocolate instant pudding
2 1/2 cups milk
Mix all together, spread over layer 2.

Layer 4
Cover layer 3 with whipped topping.

Layer 5
Sprinkle nuts on top.

Refrigerate.

KRISTINA KRIZMAN EDLEMAN—*BS '82*
Model
Savannah, Georgia

Isiah Thomas
Professional basketball player, Detroit Pistons

Isiah's Favorite Cheesecake

Crust:
3/4 cup graham cracker crumbs
1/4 cup ground walnuts
1/2 teaspoon cinnamon
1/2 cup melted butter

Mix all ingredients in spring form pan and pat down on bottom.

Filling:
3 beaten eggs
1 cup sugar
2 8-ounce packages cream cheese (softened)
1/4 teaspoon salt
2 teaspoons vanilla
1/2 teaspoon almond extract
3 cups sour cream

Blend all ingredients together in mixer. Pour in pan and bake at 300° for 50-60 minutes.

Turn oven off and open door slightly. Leave cake in oven an additional 40 minutes.

Remove and refrigerate overnight.

ISIAH THOMAS—*BA '87*
Professional Basketball Player, Detroit Pistons
Royal Oak, Michigan

"The only thing as sweet and satisfying as this cake is a victory over Purdue!"

—L.L.L.

Chambourd Flourless Chocolate Cake with Raspberry Sauce

Cake:

1 cup unsalted butter
1/2 pound bittersweet or semisweet chocolate
1 cup cocoa
1 1/2 cups sugar
6 eggs, slightly beaten
1/3 cup Chambourd, Framboise, or raspberry flavored liqueur

Preheat oven to 350°. Grease a 9-inch round deep cake pan or springform pan; line bottom with a circle of wax paper or parchment paper and grease the paper. If using a springform pan, cover the outside bottom and sides with foil to prevent water from seeping in through the seam.

Melt butter and chocolate in the top of a double boiler, stirring occasionally. Remove from heat and allow to cool. In a large bowl, mix cocoa and sugar, add eggs and mix to combine. Stir in the butter and chocolate mixture and the liqueur. Pour into cake pan and place cake pan inside larger pan. Fill outer pan with hot water to a depth of one inch, being careful not to splash water into the chocolate mixture.

Bake for 40 to 45 minutes or until top is firm to the touch. Remove cake pan from water and cool on a wire rack. Run knife along sides before removing from pan. Invert on a serving dish, leaving parchment or wax paper on top. Cover with plastic wrap and refrigerate several hours or overnight.

To serve, remove from refrigerator and peel off parchment or wax paper. Cut in small slices (it is very rich) and serve each slice in a pool of raspberry sauce. (recipe follows) Drizzle additional raspberry sauce over top if desired. Keep leftover refrigerated or wrap tightly and freeze.

Raspberry Sauce

Thaw two 10-ounce packages of frozen raspberries in syrup. Puree berries and juice, in blender or food processor, until smooth. Strain to remove seeds, if desired. Add raspberry liqueur; add some superfine sugar to taste, if desired. Blend thoroughly. Sauce will not be too sweet, as the tartness provides a contrast to the rich chocolate.

LINDA L. LIPP—*BA '76*
Freelance writer
North Chicago, Illinois

"These are great appetizers and can be cut larger for luncheon squares."

—E.P.H.

Greek Spinach Bites

1 package ready-made pie crusts
2 packages frozen chopped spinach, well-drained (squeeze out water)
4 large eggs
10 ounces jack cheese, diced
8 ounces feta cheese, crumbled
1 cup plain yogurt

1/2 cup milk
1/2 cup flour
1/4 cup oil
2 tablespoons lemon juice
2 or 3 green onions, sliced
pinch of each of dill, nutmeg, and cayenne pepper
1/2 cup parmesan cheese

Take a large cookie sheet that has an edge about 1 inch high and line it with the pie crusts, cutting and shaping where necessary to cover the entire sheet.

Beat the eggs, and add the yogurt, mixing till smooth. Add all the other ingredients, except the parmesan cheese, and stir until it is all well mixed.

Pour the filling into the crust and smooth it down so the crust is evenly filled. Sprinkle the top with a moderately generous amount of parmesan.

Bake 50-60 minutes at 350° until it is brown and puffy. Cool and cut into 1 1/2 or 2-inch squares, and then cut on the diagonal to make triangles.

ELAINE PODBER HANEY—*BS '80*
Owner, Silly Whimz, and
MT, project supervisor, Evanston Hospital
Skokie, Illinois

"At ten years of age, this was the first cookie recipe I ever collected. It came from a neighbor who was nicknamed "Cookie" Larsen for her great creations. These also freeze well."

—E.P.H.

Million Dollar Cookies

1/2 cup brown sugar
1/2 cup white sugar
1/4 cup shortening
1/4 cup margarine
1 egg
1/4 teaspoon baking soda
1/4 teaspoon vanilla
2 cups sifted all-purpose flour
1/2 cup finely chopped pecans

Cream together sugars and margarine and shortening until fluffy. Add egg, lightly beaten, and blend well. Add soda and flour, mixing well. Lastly mix in pecans.

Taking batter by the teaspoon, roll into little balls and place on a greased cookie sheet. Take a small water glass or juice glass and rub on the batter so it gets slightly greasy. Dip the glass bottom into a bowl of sugar. For Christmas cookies, use red or green tinted sugar (granulated sugar works better than large crystal decorative sugar). Punch down each dough ball with the sugared glass. You need to dip into sugar in between each cookie.

Bake in a pre-heated 350° oven for 10 minutes. Makes about 3 dozen.

ELAINE PODBER HANEY—*BS '80*
Owner, Silly Whimz, and
MT, project supervisor, Evanston Hospital
Skokie, Illinois

Isiah Thomas drives hard down the court for another basket.

"Terrific for tailgate parties and perfect for potlucks."
—E.P.H.

Elaine's Pig-Out Pasta Salad

10 to 16 ounces (or more) dry pasta ***(I like to use tri-color twists)***
1 or 2 cans pitted black olives
1 can plain, or 2 jars marinated, artichoke hearts, cut in fourths
1 pint cherry tomatoes, cut in half
1 red or sweet onion, chopped in large pieces or 1 bunch green onions, sliced
about 1/2 bunch broccoli, blanched
about 1/2 head cauliflower, blanched (optional)

(NOTE: Other vegetables that are good to include are: red pepper or a jar of pimentos, green pepper, pea pods mushrooms, carrots, or whatever is around and strikes your fancy. You can use all of these or none of these—it differs every time.)

1/2–1 pound provolone, fontina, gouda, or any other cheese you like, cut up into cubes or small sticks
1/2 cup olive oil
1/2 cup corn oil
3/4 cups (about) red wine or herb vinegar
2 to 3 tablespoons dried oregano
2 teaspoon dried basil ***(you can use fresh, but go easy with it)***
2 teaspoons garlic powder ***(fresh garlic is too strong)***
1/4 cup parmesan cheese

TO BLANCH VEGETABLES: Bring a large pot of water to a full boil and cook or steam vegetables 3–5 minutes, depending on the type of veggie, they should still be crunchy. Immediately put veggies into sink or pot full of ice water to stop cooking and preserve color.

TO COOK PASTA: Follow package directions, but undercook somewhat. As pasta sits in the vinaigrette and soaks up the oil, it will "cook" more and become very mushy if it is not al dente. Pasta should also be put into ice cold water once it is cooked and drained.

TO MAKE DRESSING: All amounts listed above for the dressing ingredients are approximate, and can be altered to please your tastebuds. As the salad sits in the refrigerator and marinates, the pasta will soak up the oil and vinegar and you may need to add more the second day, especially oil. You don't want to use all olive oil, because the flavor will be overpowering, but some olive oil gives a nice taste. To vary the dressing you can try adding a little mayonnaise or dijon mustard, but I just like mine with lots of oregano!

HINTS: Make the pasta salad the day before you want to serve it, and you won't be as tired the day of your party, plus it will taste better. If you choose to add mushrooms, do it the morning of the day you will be serving the salad, they tend to get discolored. For a change of pace, try an antipasto salad by adding sliced pepperoni or salami, along with some pepperoncini.

ELAINE PODBER HANEY—*BS '80*
Owner, Silly Whimz, and
MT, project supervisor, Evanston Hospital
Skokie, Illinois

"I've never had to worry about leftovers with this dip."
—E.P.H.

Elaine's Deluxe Guacamole

4-6 ripe fresh avocados
1 package frozen Mexican-style avocado dip
2 medium tomatoes, seeds removed; peel if desired
1 medium-large red onion
2 small cans sliced olives
1/4-1/2 cup chopped fresh cilantro if available (also called coriander or Chinese parsley)
2-3 tablespoons sour cream
2-3 tablespoons mayonnaise
1 tablespoon cumin powder (not a hot spice), or to taste
chopped jalapeños, cayenne pepper, or red pepper sauce to taste
lemon juice to taste
8–12 ounces shredded cheddar cheese for topping

Chop tomatoes and onions into medium-small pieces. Mix together all other ingredients, except cheese, 1 can of olives, spices and lemon juice. Add some lemon juice and spices to taste, but remember dip will get hotter as it sits. You may not want to add spice if you prefer a milder dip. To scale down recipe, you can use 2 fresh avocados, but then you should buy plain frozen avocado dip and add your own spices, because the Mexican-style will make it too hot for most people. Before topping, add a thin layer of lemon juice over the top to retard discoloring. Then top with cheese and 1 can of the olives and ENJOY!

ELAINE PODBER HANEY—*BS '80*
Owner, Silly Whimz, and
MT, project supervisor, Evanston Hospital
Skokie, Illinois

"Lentil loaf...is generally served as a main dish, but...is also good on sandwiches as a leftover."

— D.A.Z.

Lentil Loaf

This dish is best complemented by a tomato sauce and served with baked potatoes and a green salad. Use leftovers for tasty sandwiches.

Boil 4 cups of water with a dash of salt and oil. Add 2 cups dry lentil beans and simmer 30 minutes or until lentils are tender.

Combine 1 cup shredded cheddar cheese, 1 cup bread crumbs, 1 diced medium onion and 6 sliced mushrooms.

Mix 2 eggs, 1/2 cup heavy cream, 1 teaspoon salt, 1/2 teaspoon pepper, 1/2 teaspoon cloves and 1/4 cup fresh chopped parsley.

Preheat oven to 350°

Butter a 10-inch tube pan.

Combine all ingredients and pour into pan, inserting a few pats of butter along the top of the mixture.

Bake for 45 minutes. Serves 6.

DEBORAH A. ZIMMERMAN Bussiere—*BS '89*
Senior marketing associate, Dean Witter
New York, New York

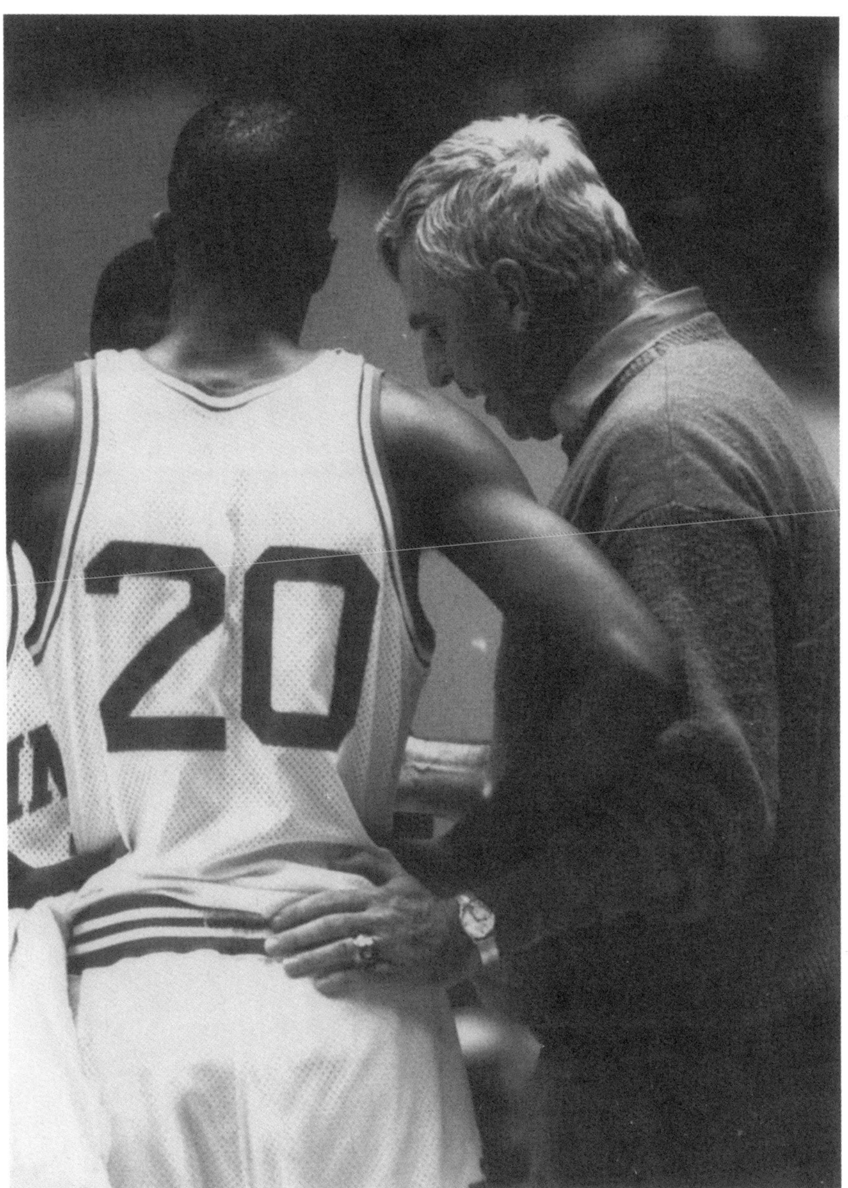

Coach Knight and a player review the game plan.

Faculty and Regional Campuses…

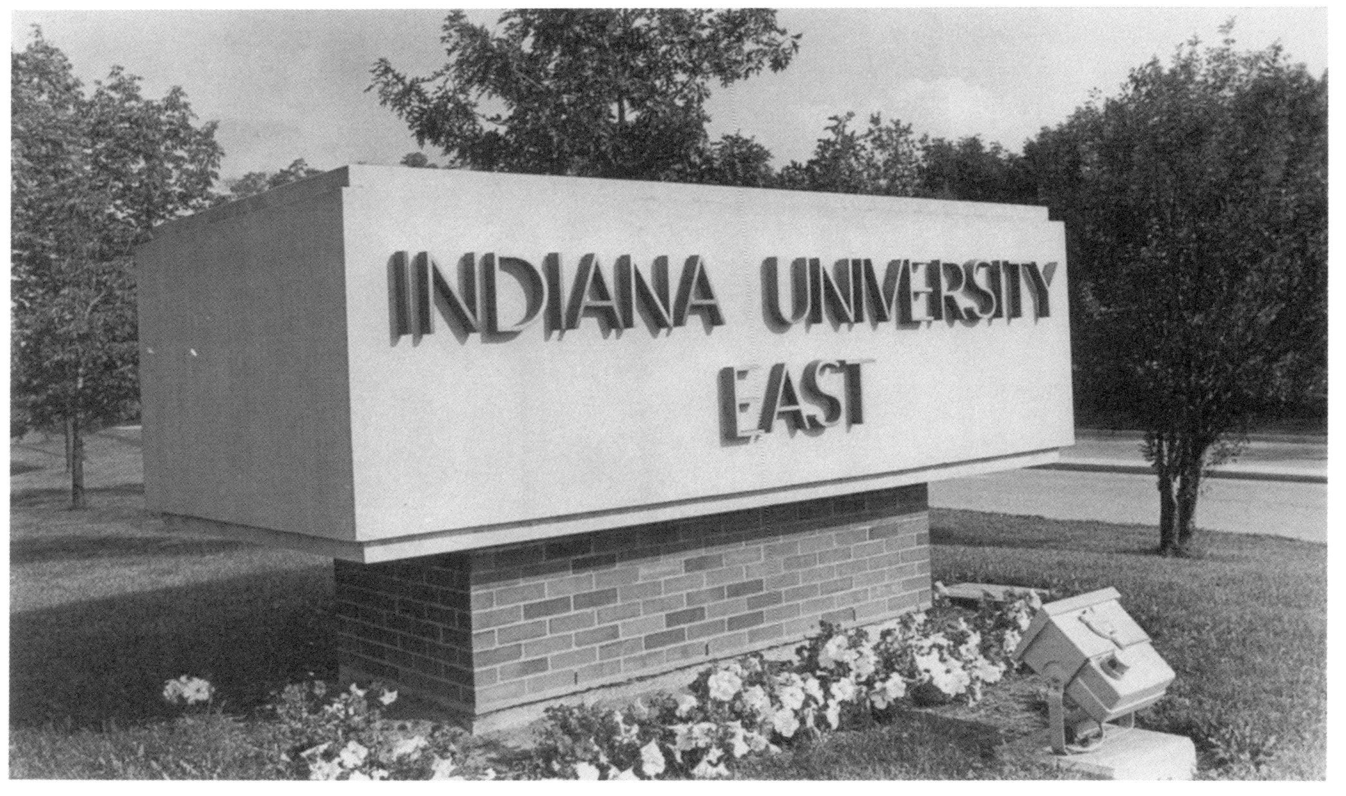

IU East campus at Richmond

Guenther's French Onion Soup

Saute 1 1/2 large white onions (cut into small bite-size pieces) with 4-6 tablespoons of butter or margarine, until the onion is transparent.

Stir in enough white flour to absorb all of the butter. Pour in 8 cups of chicken broth, stirring constantly until the flour dissolves. Add 1 tablespoon poppy seed. Add salt and pepper to taste. Add more chicken broth or consommé for soup richness. Add 1/4 cup sherry or white wine prior to serving.

Pour soup over a grated mild cheese and float a piece of fresh toast on the soup.

JOHN GUENTHER
Associate Professor, Fine Arts
IU Southeast

Chicken Casserole

1 frying chicken, boiled and boned
1 can French cut green beans, with half of juice
1 can cream of celery soup
1 can water chestnuts, sliced
1 package curried rice or bought noodles
1 small onion, finely chopped
1 cup mayonnaise
3 cups chicken broth

Cook rice or noodles in chicken broth until done. Add onion and cook 5 more minutes. Mix rest of ingredients and add to rice or noodles. Pour into a buttered dish. Top with bread or cracker crumbs. Bake at 350° for 40 minutes.

EMMA PEARCE
Associate Professor, Nursing
IU Kokomo

"An old recipe in my family, but fit even for royalty coming to breakfast!"

—R.S.

Shaver's Famous Dried Beef Gravy

6 ounces smoked dried beef, sliced and chopped
1 4-ounce can of mushroom pieces (may substitute fresh mushrooms)
1 stick (4 ounces) margarine or butter
5 cups milk
4 eggs, hard-boiled and chopped
6 ounces sharp cheddar cheese, slivered or shredded
1/2 cup cooked green peas (optional)
2/3 cup cornstarch and water thickening seasonings
6 English muffins, split and toasted

In a 10-inch skillet, saute beef and mushrooms together in margarine or butter. Remove skillet from heat and cool slightly. Add milk. Return to heat and add eggs, cheese and peas (optional). Season to taste, using an all-purpose mix and generous dash of curry powder. Bring to a boil over moderate heat, stirring frequently, and stir in enough of the cornstarch and water mixture to make a thick gravy. Simmer for two or three minutes.

Serve by ladling generous portions of the hot gravy mixture over the split muffins. Serves six or more.

ROBERT SHAVER
Professor Emeritus, Geology
IU Bloomington

Broiled Scallops

24 ounces scallops
4 tablespoons of butter or margarine
4 tablespoons lemon juice
1 teaspoon salt
1 teaspoon Worcestershire sauce
1/2 teaspoon dried tarragon
1/2 teaspoon dried basil

Put everything but the scallops in a small bowl. Spread half the mixture on the scallops after they have been put in a single layer on a broiler-proof dish or pan. Broil the scallops close to the broiler flame for 3 minutes. Turn the scallops and cover with remaining sauce and finish broiling—approximately 2 minutes.

Serve with herbed rice. Serves 4.

ROY SCHREIBER
Professor, History
IU South Bend

Hot Chops Casserole

1 6 1/2-ounce box wild and white rice, uncooked
1 cup diced red and green jalapeños or pickled hot peppers
1 cup onions, diced
1 cup celery, diced
1 8-ounce can undrained mushrooms (or 2 cans, if desired)
1 10-ounce can cream of mushroom soup
1 cup milk
6 pork chops
salt and pepper

Brown pork chops. Mix rice, peppers, onions, celery and mushrooms. Place mix in greased 12 x 9-inch glass baking dish.

Top with browned chops and pour soup and milk over all.

Bake 1 hour at 350°.

Down-Home Vegetable Beef Soup

1 1/2 quarts beef broth
6 potatoes, peeled and cubed
1 turnip, peeled and diced
1 large carrot, sliced
1 stalk celery, sliced
1/2 cup dried beans, any type
1/4 cup dried barley
2 cups green beans, cut
1 28-ounce can tomatoes, including juice
1 medium onion, quartered and sliced
1 cup zucchini, sliced
1 or 2 jalapeño peppers, minced

2 green onions, cut in 1-inch slices
1/2 cup lemon juice
1/4 cup vinegar
1 28-ounce can chunk beef (and gravy)
2 tablespoons parsley
1 teaspoon basil
anything left in the garden or refrigerator
salt and pepper to taste

Add in order given in large stock pot. Bring to a boil, then low boil until vegetables are done and flavors mixed well. Keeps well and flavor improves. May add other favorite vegetables, 1 cup wine, to taste. Serve to hungry horde with crackers, cornbread, or crusty bread.

CLIFFORD SCOTT
Associate Professor, History
IU Fort Wayne

"Big Red" Eggs

1 dozen eggs, hard boiled
beet juice from red beets

add:
1 cup vinegar
1 cup sugar
1 teaspoon red food coloring
1/2 teaspoon salt

Bring to a boil; pour over eggs. Marinate over night.

"Big Red" eggs will appear!

GEORGE MALACINSKI
Professor/Biology
IU Bloomington

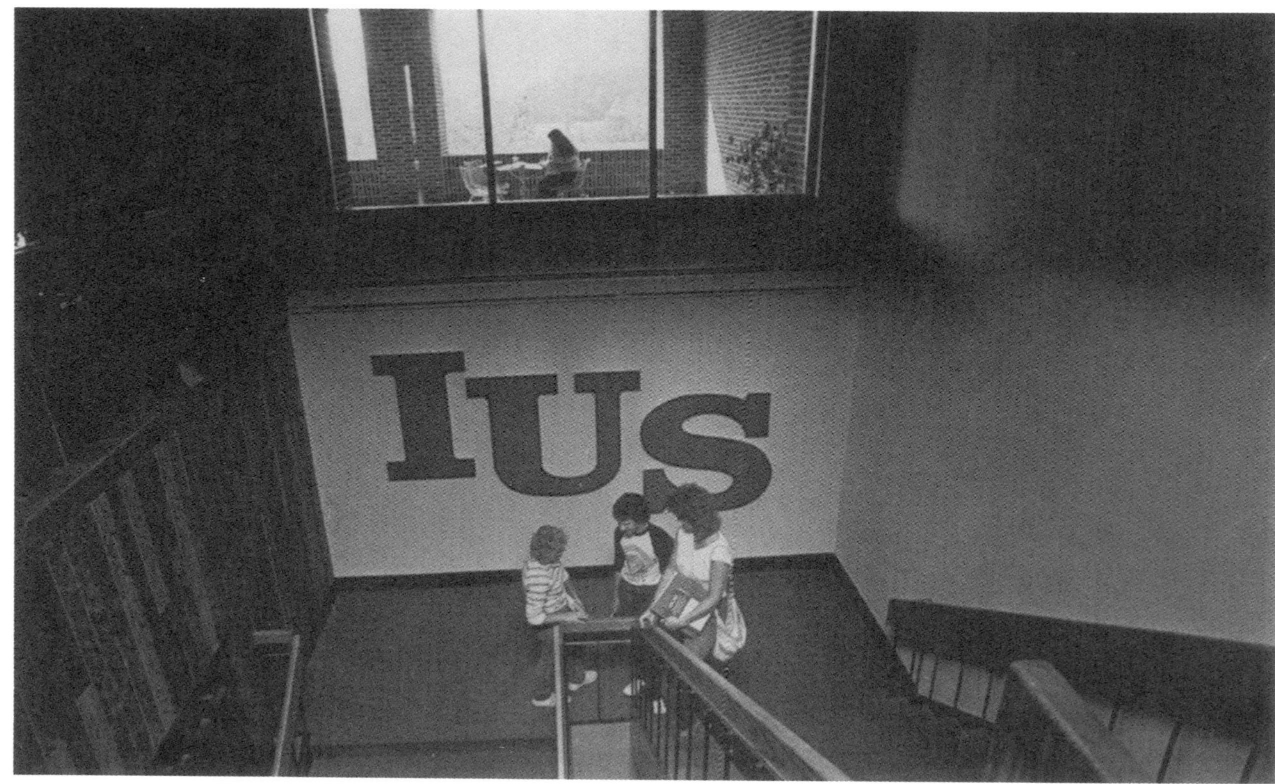

IUS at New Albany in southeastern Indiana.

Spanish Rice

4 cups cooked rice
2 cups canned tomatoes (cut into small pieces)
1 cup tomato sauce (or 4 ounces tomato paste and 4 ounces water)
1/2 pound bacon
1/2 pound grated cheddar cheese (preferably sharp)
1/2 cup chopped onion
1/2 cup chopped green or sweet red pepper
1/2 teaspoon salt (optional)
1/2 teaspoon cayenne pepper

Fry bacon; remove fat and cut into small pieces.
Brown onions and peppers in small amount of bacon fat. Add tomatoes, tomato sauce or paste and water, spices, bacon.

Cook for five minutes at low temperature.

Add cooked rice to other ingredients, stir. Cover with grated cheese and cook at low temperature in a covered frying pan until cheese is melted (about 5 minutes).

Serves 4 to 6 persons.

PAUL SCHERER
Professor, History
IU South Bend

Manicotti with Cheese

1 box (12-16 ounces) manicotti shells
1 pound part-skim ricotta cheese
6-8 ounces shredded mozzarella
32 ounces homemade (or store-bought) spaghetti sauce

Boil manicotti according to package directions. Pour half the spaghetti sauce into a rectangular baking dish. Mix together ricotta and mozzarella. Fill the shells with the cheese mixture (a healthy teaspoon per shell) Place them in a single layer on the spaghetti sauce.

Cover with the remaining sauce, taking care to moisten each shell. Top with some parmesan.

Bake, covered, for 50 minutes in a 350° oven.

Uncover the last 5 or 10 minutes.

Serves a family of four for two days.

MARJORIE HERSHEY
Professor, Political Science
IU Bloomington

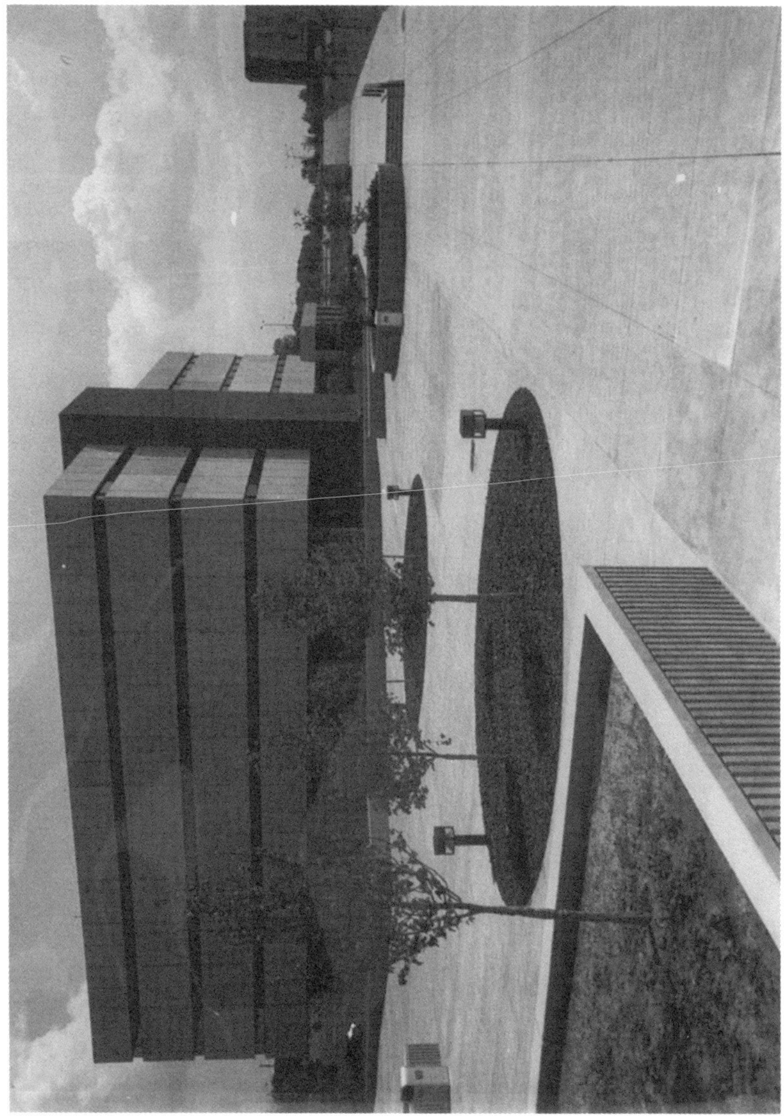

IU Fort Wayne

Quick and Delicious

1 fresh green pepper
handful fresh mushrooms
1 tablespoon olive oil
1 or 2 cloves garlic
salt
pepper
nutmeg
fresh cream or evaporated milk (optional)

Peel and mince the garlic and saute lightly in olive oil. Seed green pepper and cut into roughly 1/2-inch squares and add to pan.

Coarsely slice washed mushrooms (an amount about equal to the pepper) and add to pan when the pepper is beginning to soften.

Season to taste, but a lot of pepper is nice.

Scrape in some fresh nutmeg.

Simmer over low heat, covered, until peppers are tender. Optional: add a little fresh cream, cook into sauce. Serve.

HAROLD LANGLAND
Professor, Fine Arts
IU South Bend

Tomato Salad

tomatoes
french dressing
chopped chives or lemon rind
segments of lemon or orange

Scald and skin the tomatoes and cut in thick slices transversely (halve if small).

Spoon over a little French dressing and scatter over a little chopped chive or shredded blanched lemon rind, and segments of lemon or orange.

Use approximately 1 tomato per person.

Can be prepared day ahead and refrigerated.

GUY HUBBARD
Professor, Education
IU Bloomington

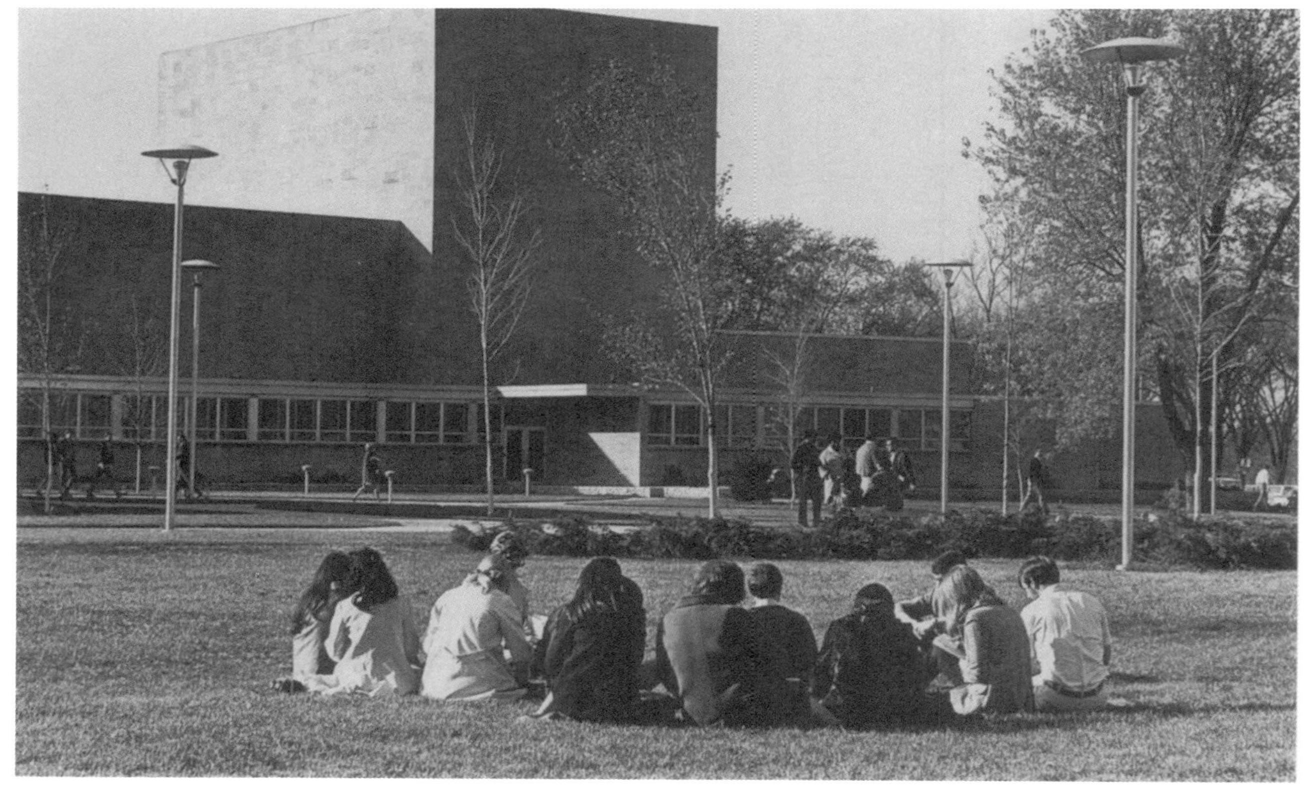

IU Northwest at Gary

Italian Zucchini

1 medium onion, chopped
2 cloves garlic, chopped
3 medium zucchini,6 to 8 inches long, sliced
2 medium tomatoes, peeled and chopped
1 teaspoon dry oregano
1 to 2 cups grated mozzarella cheese
salt and pepper to taste

Slice a medium onion and 2 cloves of garlic into a large skillet. Saute in 2 tablespoons olive oil.

Slice two medium zucchini squash or several small ones into skillet.

Add 3 medium tomatoes, chopped, and with skin removed. Add 1 teaspoon dry oregano or 1 tablespoon chopped fresh oregano (Oreganum herculaneum). Saute until squash is soft.

Just before serving, add 1 cup grated mozzarella cheese and allow it to melt.

N. GARY LANE
Professor, Geology
IU Bloomington

"Maui no ka oi."

—G.C.

Ribs Lahaina

ribs and tenderloin
1 large onion, sliced
2 lemons, sliced
salt and pepper

Brown for 30 minutes in 450° oven

Sauce:
1 bottle beer
3/4 cup catsup
2 tablespoon vinegar
2 tablespoon Worcestershire
3 drops hot red pepper sauce
1/4 cup brown sugar

Combine sauce ingredients in saucepan, simmer 2 minutes

Add sauce to meat and baste every 15 minutes in 350° oven for about 1 hour.

DR. GEORGE CAVANAGH
Associate Professor, Music
IU Fort Wayne

Summer Perfection

2 envelopes unflavored gelatin
1/2 cup cold water
12 ounces cream cheese
6 tablespoons sugar
2 cups milk
1 cup boiling water
2 6-ounce cans frozen lemonade, thawed
1 quart strawberries

Use two quart mold or 7 individual molds.

Soften gelatin in cold water, then dissolve in boiling water. In another bowl, blend with an electric mixer the cream cheese and sugar, gradually adding milk.

Add gelatin to cream cheese mixture, add lemonade and blend.

Pour into mold and refrigerate until jelled. Unmold and fill center with strawberries.

MERYL ENGLANDER
Professor, Educational Psychology
IU Bloomington

Broccoli and Rice Casserole

3 cups cooked rice
1 large package chopped broccoli (20 ounces)

Cook broccoli with small onion, some celery, green peppers (all chopped). Drain when done.

To the above, add 1 large jar Cheese Whiz and mix well. Put in a long baking dish and bake at 350° until bubbly, about 20-30 minutes.

Garnish with paprika.

JOHN B. DROSTE
Professor, Geology
IU Bloomington

Lucky Thirteen Italian Dressing

Mix the following ingredients in a salad dressing bottle:

1/2 teaspoon salt
1 tablespoon sugar
1/4 teaspoon dry mustard
1/4 teaspoon paprika
1/4 teaspoon onion salt
1/2 teaspoon parsley flakes
1/4 teaspoon oregano
1/2 clove garlic, or to taste
1/8 teaspoon black pepper

Then add:

2 tablespoons cider vinegar
3/8 cup olive oil
1 tablespoon red wine garlic vinegar
1 teaspoon lemon juice

Refrigerate and allow to blend before using.

B. EDWARD McCLELLAN
Associate Professor, Education
IU Bloomington

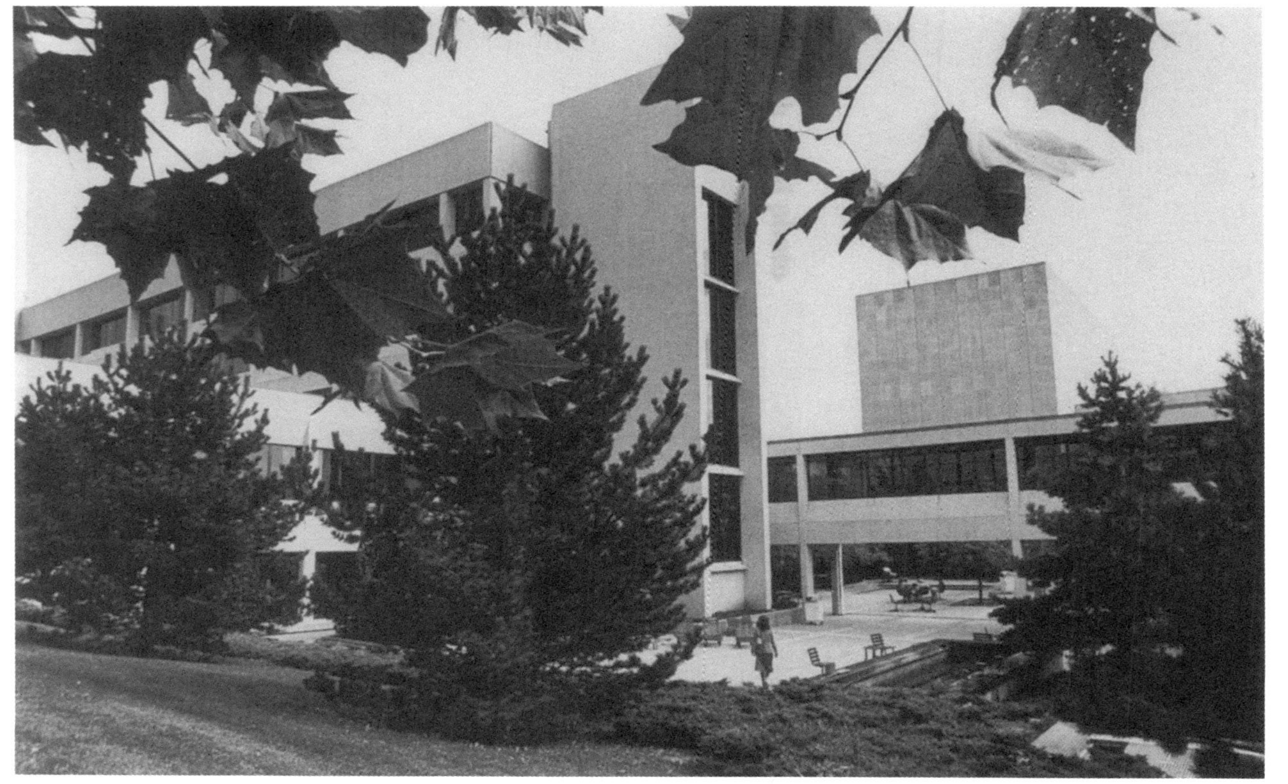

IU South Bend

Rice Casserole

1 cup rice, raw
1 pound jack cheese, grated
1 pint sour cream
1 4-ounce can chopped green chili peppers

Layer rice and other ingredients (after cooking rice) in a buttered casserole, end with grated cheese on top.

Bake, covered, 30 minutes at 350°.

Serves 6

Can be prepared in advance.

SUSANN McDONALD
Professor, Music
IU Bloomington

Casserole Recipe

1 quart cooked beans (three cans)
1 1/4 cups bean liquid
1 cup chopped ripe olives
1 teaspoon salt
1 tablespoon cornstarch
1 garlic clove, minced
1 cup chopped green pepper
1 cup chopped onion
1 tablespoon chili powder
1/2 cup grated cheese (your choice)
1/4 cup salad oil

Saute chopped onion and green pepper in salad oil. To liquid from beans, add olives, garlic, salt, chili powder, cornstarch and heat.

Combine all ingredients and put in casserole.

Bake 30 minutes at 375°.

Put grated cheese on top and heat until melted.

BURCHARD DAVIDSON
Professor Emeritus, Political Science
IU Kokomo

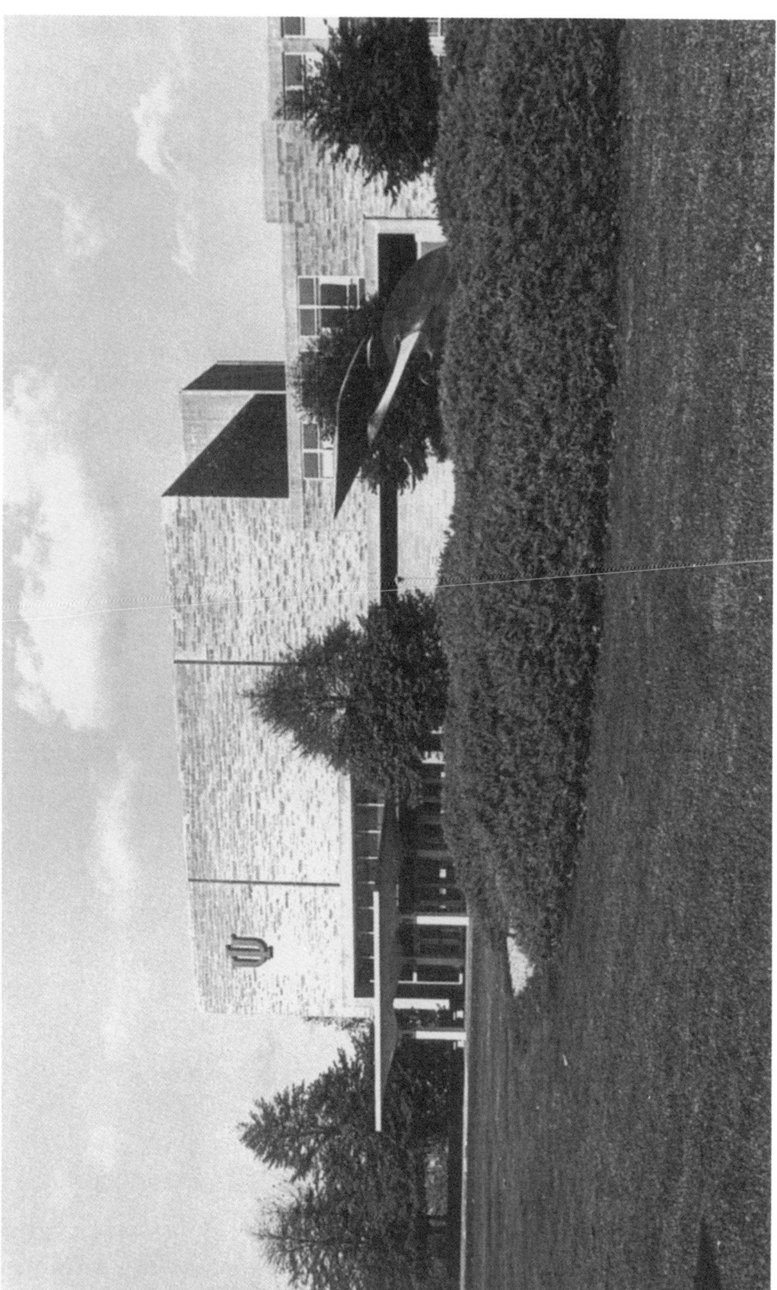

IU Kokomo

"These rolls are always a hit at opening night cast parties."

—D.W.

Mashed Potato Rolls

1 package yeast dissolved in
1/2 cup lukewarm water (105°-110°)
1 cup scalded and cooled milk
1 cup mashed Irish potatoes (no lumps—cooled)
1/2 cup shortening
1/2 cup sugar
1 teaspoon salt
2 well beaten eggs
5 to 6 cups all-purpose or bread flour

Combine milk, potatoes, shortening, sugar and salt. Add to the yeast.

Add beaten eggs and 11/2 cups flour. Beat well and let set in a warm oven for 30 minutes. Add the remainder of flour, a small amount at a time (Dough will become too thick to mix with a spoon, so mix by hand and knead until smooth). Put in a greased bowl and place in warm place to rise.

When double in size, remove and knead.

Let rise again. Knead again.

(NOTE: At this stage it can be made into rolls or refrigerated for later use.)

Let rolls rise to double. Bake 30 minutes in a 350° preheated oven.

DOROTHY WEBB
Professor, Communication and Theater
IUPUI Indianapolis

Cookie Recipe

2 eggs
1 cup solid shortening
1 1/2 cups sugar
1/4 cup milk
1 teaspoon vanilla
4 cups flour (not heaping)
1 teaspoon soda
2 teaspoons baking powder
pinch salt
pinch nutmeg

Combine soda, baking powder, and flour. Cream sugar, shortening, and eggs. Add dry ingredients, milk and vanilla.

Bake at 375° for 8 minutes or until slightly brown.

Icing

1 box powdered sugar (16 ounces)
1 small package cream cheese
1 stick butter

ARTHUR D. BRILL
Professor, Education
IUPUI Indianapolis

Italian, Chunky Style

1 can pitted ripe olives, drained
1/2 to 1 pound salami, cut into bite-size cubes
1/2 to 1 pound brick cheese, cut into bite-size chunks
7 or 8 stalks of celery, cut into bite-size chunks

Combine and cover with vinegar and oil or Italian dressing.

Great with lasagna.

R. BRUCE McQUIGG
Associate Professor, Education
IU Bloomington

Ad Lib Anti-Waste Casserole

Miscellaneous leftovers
pasta
1 or 2 eggs
stock and/or milk
spices and cheese

1. Boil, but not until completely cooked, the appropriate amount of pasta.

2. Mix the incompletely cooked pasta with the other ingredients except for the cheese, using just enough liquid to make it agreeably mushy.

3. Grease a baking dish, add the mixture, and top with cheese.

4. Bake at about 350° until the cheese is thoroughly melted.

VICTOR WALLIS
Associate Professor, Political Science
IUPUI Indianapolis

Barbecued Spareribs

2 to 3 pounds country-style ribs
1/2 cup catsup
1 1/2 teaspoon salt
1/4 teaspoon hot red pepper sauce
1/8 teaspoon chili powder
1 cup water
1/2 teaspoon mustard
1 tablespoon brown sugar

Put ribs in Dutch oven. Mix remaining ingredients and pour over ribs. Slice 1/2 onion and cover ribs.

Bake, covered, at 325° for 2 1/2 hours, uncovering during the last 1/2 hour to thicken sauce.

L. KEVIN KASTENS
Assistant Professor, Music
IU Bloomington

"Give that tailgate party an international flair."

—J.M.S.

Catalan Garlic Bread

Start with a loaf of European peasant-style bread. Otherwise use slices of lightly toasted French bread. Bread should be dry and strong enough not to turn into mush.

Rub gently with garlic (unpeeled cloves cut in half work best). One or both sides, according to taste.

Rub a little less gently with ripe tomato (cut in half, also, of course). One side only, now.

Sprinkle wisely with salt.

Sprinkle generously with olive oil. From Catalonia preferably.

Eat with country ham, or cheese, or cold cuts, sausage, anchovies or in its magnificent end-of-summer self.

JOSEP MIQUEL SOBRER
Professor, Spanish and Portuguese
IU Bloomington

Enchiladas Camarones

1 dozen corn tortillas
1 can chopped green chiles
2 small packages of frozen small size shrimp
1 bottle mild green taco sauce
1 bottle mild red taco sauce
2 eggs
1 pound Monterey jack cheese
1 pint cholesterol free oil
2 teaspoons olive oil

Prepare tortillas by frying in oil for 5 - 10 seconds on each side and drain on paper towels.

Thaw shrimp by placing packages in hot water. Add 2 eggs, chopped chiles, 1/2 pound grated cheese and shrimp to large mixing bowl and mix thoroughly.

Grease bottom and sides of a large oven-proof baking dish with olive oil. Add about 2 tablespoons of stuffing mix to each tortilla and roll up and place in baking dish.

Grate remaining cheese over rolled tortillas and spread evenly. Add taco sauce to top in alternate rows of red and green stripes parallel to long axis of dish.

Bake in oven preheated to 350° for 40 minutes and serve.

RUSSELL A. BONHAM
Professor, Chemistry
IU Bloomington

Cauliflower Croquettes

1 fresh cauliflower
1 egg
2 tablespoons olive oil
1/2 teaspoon salt

Cut cauliflower into pieces and steam until soft. Beat white of egg, mix with yolk and add salt. Dip the steamed cauliflower pieces in the egg.

In a skillet, heat oil on medium high heat. Place cauliflower in skillet and fry until golden or light brown, about 6 to 10 minutes.

Makes 4 servings.

MARTHE ROSENFELD
Associate Professor, French
IU Fort Wayne

Carnot's Casserole (*"C.C."*)

1 pound lean ground beef
1 large onion chopped
1 can corn, drained
1 can spaghetti sauce
2 cups large pasta noodles, such as mostacciola or rigatoni, cooked
cayenne pepper, black pepper, to taste
dash of chili powder, to taste

Brown meat and onion together then drain off fat. Add corn,

spaghetti sauce and enough cayenne pepper to make a warm glow. Stir in cooked pasta.

Optional: Add 1 cup sharp cheddar cheese and melt it before adding pasta.

FREDERICK THATCHER
Associate Professor, Physics
IUPUI Indianapolis

Zucchini Salad

4 medium zucchinis
2 green onions
1 green pepper
1 celery rib
2 carrots, thinly sliced
1/3 cup sugar
1/3 cup white vinegar
3 tablespoons vegetable oil
1/2 teaspoon salt

Slice zucchini in about 1/8-inch slices. Slice onions and peppers thinly. Coarsely chop celery. Thinly slice carrots.

Beat together sugar, vinegar, oil and salt in blender until well mixed. Pour over vegetables and gently toss to coat. Cover with plastic wrap and refrigerate several hours or overnight. Salad will stay fresh at least 2 days.

JAMES WALDEN
Professor Emeritus, Education
IU Bloomington

Fruited Meatloaf

2 pounds very lean ground beef
1 1/2 cups peeled apple
1 1/2 cup peeled pear (or 4 dried pears)
1 large onion
1 cup any type breadcrumbs
1/2 cup pecans
4 large eggs
1 1/2 teaspoons salt
1 tablespoon paprika
1/2 teaspoon each of sage, nutmeg, allspice
1 tablespoon molasses

Put nuts and onions in food processor. Process. Add remaining ingredients. Process well.

Pack in loaf or circle pan.

Bake at 350° 1 1/4 hours.

Chill thoroughly and slice.

JORDAN LEIBMAN
Professor, Business Law
IUPUI Indianapolis

Eggplant Casserole

1 large eggplant
1/2 Valencia onion
1 pound mozzarella cheese
mushrooms
oregano

Slice eggplant, onions, mushrooms and cheese into thin slabs.

Line casserole with oil.

Layer the slabs: eggplant, onion, oregano, cheese, eggplant, mushrooms, oregano, cheese, eggplant, onions, oregano, cheese, etc. Finish with layer of cheese on top.

Cook for 45 minutes at 350°.

Tomatoes, hot peppers, other versions are possible and recommended. Serves four to six.

JOHN D. BARLOW
Dean, School of Liberal Arts
IUPUI Indianapolis

Szekely Goulash

1 1/2 pounds lean leg of pork or pork shoulder
2 tablespoons all-purpose flour
2 teaspoons all-purpose flour
2 teaspoons paprika
1 1/2 teaspoons salt
2 tablespoons fat

2 tablespoons finely chopped onion
3 tablespoons hot water
1 27-ounce can sauerkraut (about 3 1/2 cups, firmly packed)
2 c ups hot water
1 1/2 cups thick sour cream

1. Set out a 4 quart sauce pot or a Dutch oven having a tight fitting cover.
2. Put lean leg of pork or pork shoulder onto wooden board and cut into 1 1/2-inch cubes.
3. To coat meat evenly, shake cubes in plastic bag containing a mixture of flour, paprika and salt. Set aside.
4. Cook fat and onion in the sauce pot over medium heat, stirring occasionally, until onion is soft.
5. Add contents of plastic bag to sauce pot; brown meat on all sides, turning occasionally. Add 3 tablespoons water.
6. Cover sauce pot and simmer 1 hour stirring occasionally; add small amounts of water as needed.
7. Shortly before end of one-hour cooking period, drain contents of can of sauerkraut.
8. If desired, rinse sauerkraut in cold water, so that the goulash will have a milder flavor; drain again. Mix sauerkraut with the meat; add 2 cups hot water.
9. Bring to boiling; cover and simmer 1/2 hour longer, or until meat is tender when pierced with a fork. Remove sauce pot from heat. Gradually blend about 1 1/2 cups cooking liquid into sour cream.
10. Blend into hot mixture. Stirring constantly, cook over low heat, 3 to 5 minutes until heated thoroughly. Do not boil.

Serve in small bowls. 6 to 8 servings.

Philip Farkas
Professor Emeritus, Music
IU Bloomington

Italian Stir-Fry Vegetables

Cut up broccoli, onions, garlic, mushrooms, celery and green peppers into small pieces. Fry at medium heat in a mixture of Italian salad dressing and olive oil (mix the proportions to suit your own taste). Serve over cooked spaghetti or noodles and sprinkle with grated cheese.

JAMES FARLOW
Associate Professor, Geology
IU Fort Wayne

Chicken Paprikash

salt and pepper to taste
2 tablespoons butter
1 cup chopped onions
1 tablespoon minced garlic
1 tablespoon sweet paprika
1/2 cup canned chicken broth
1 cup sour cream
1 tablespoon flour

Brown with butter, sprinkle onion and garlic all over, paprika over. Add chicken broth, cover, simmer until chicken is cooked. Take out and put flour in sour cream and stir into pan mixture.

If for a large group of people, mix all together and put in oven to bake and add sour cream with flour separately into the sauce and put back into the oven.

Serve with large egg noodles. (Put oleo in the boiling water to avoid sticky noodles). Makes four servings.

NORMA CHASKA
Professor, Nursing
IUPUI Indianaplis

Bok Choy Soup

1 bunch bok choy
1 bunch scallions
2 tablespoons rice wine (or white wine)
1 pound raw chicken, cut into small pieces
1 package rice noodles
3 tablespoons soy sauce or tamari
6 cups chicken broth
radishes or water chestnuts

Separate green leaves from white stems of bok choy. Chop white stems and scallions. Simmer in wine 3–5 minutes. Add raw chicken, chopped greens from bok choy and rice noodles.

Cover with boiling broth. Cover and cook 3–5 minutes. Add soy or tamari, salt to taste.

Garnish with radishes or water chestnuts.

ROBERT DICK
Professor, Communication and Theater
IUPUI Indianapolis

Patate Arrosto Della Nonna

(Roast Potatoes Grandma's style)

from Southern Italy—Anzano di Puglia

6 medium size potatoes
2 onions
salt
pepper
garlic powder
oregano (or rosemary)
olive oil
grated parmesan cheese
peeled tomatoes (small can)

Preheat oven to 400°.

Peel and cut potatoes lengthwise into eighths. Slice onions into fairly large pieces. Place in a large bowl. Season with salt, pepper, garlic powder, oregano (or rosemary) and mix well. Add parmesan cheese and mix again. Add enough olive oil to wet potatoes and mix. Spread in a casserole (preferably clay or ceramic). Add enough olive oil over the mixture to cover bottom of pan.

Break peeled tomatoes over the top of the potatoes.

Roast in oven approximately 35-45 minutes until tender and brown, turning periodically. During the last 5-10 minutes of roasting place under broiler to crisp.

To hurry roasting time, cover casserole with tin foil, then place under broiler to brown and crisp.

EDOARDO LEBANO
Professor, French and Italian
IU Bloomington

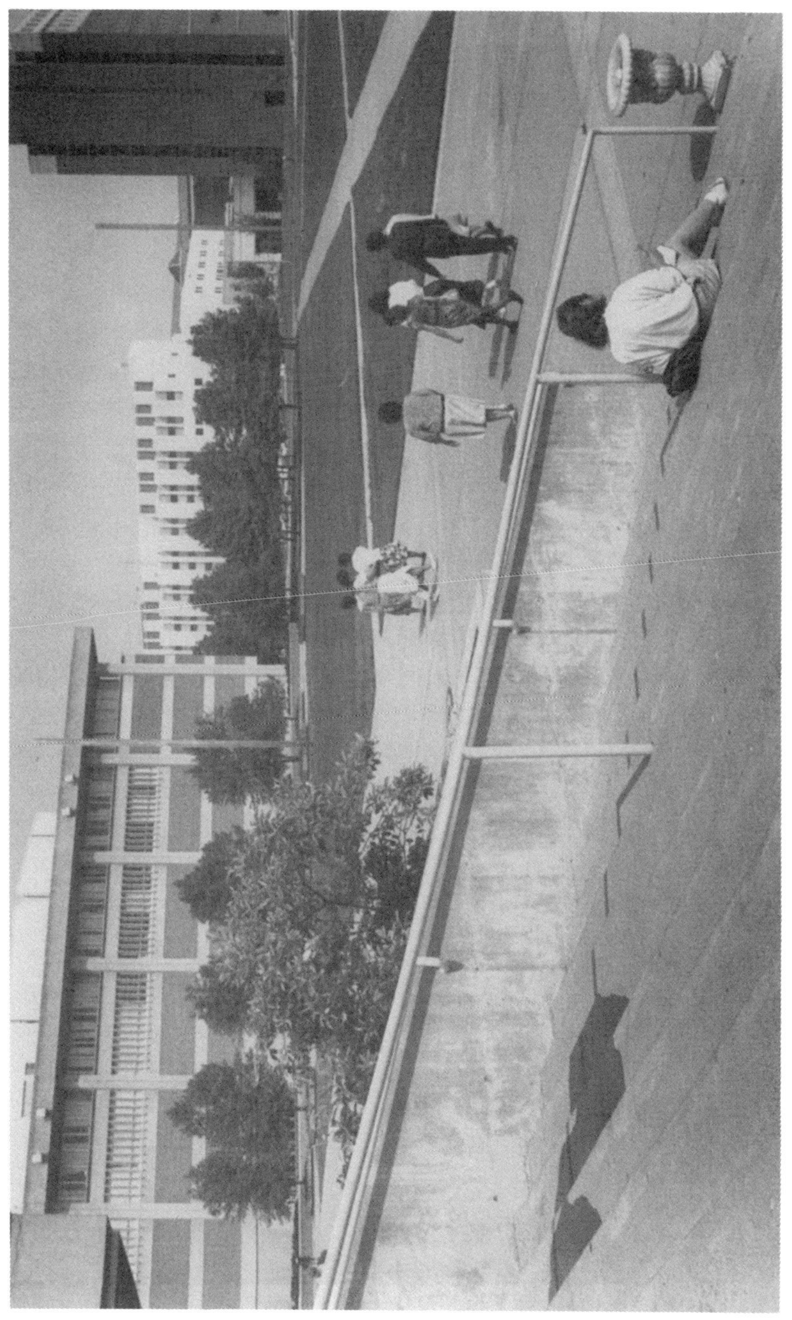

IUPUI—the successful teaming of IU and Purdue in Indianapolis.

Zucchini in Forno al Formaggio

10 medium size zucchini squash
3 cups milk
1 cup flour
1/3 cup olive oil
1/2 stick butter
1 can peeled tomatoes
10 slices provolone cheese (sweet)
salt and pepper

Wash the zucchini and dry them. then cut them in four parts lengthwise; put them for ten minutes in a bowl full of milk in which you have added a bit of salt. Drain them and flour them. In a frying pan heat oil and fry zucchini. Once fried, place the zucchini in an oven-proof casserole with some melted butter. Cover the first layer of zucchini with small slices of butter, some pieces of peeled tomatoes and the provolone cheese. Sprinkle some pepper on top. Then do the same for the second layer. Cover the top layer with the cheese and place casserole in a 350° oven for 10-15 minutes. Serves 5.

EDOARDO LEBANO
Professor, French and Italian
IU Bloomington

Penne ai Quattro Formaggi

1/4 pound gorgonzola cheese
1/4 pound fontina cheese
1/4 pound asiago cheese
1/2 cup parmesan cheese
2 tablespoons butter
2 tablespoons parsley, finely chopped
salt and black pepper to taste
1 pound penne

***Optional*:**
1 shot brandy
1/3 cup milk
2 tablespoons cream cheese

In a skillet melt the butter, then add the gorgonzola cheese breaking it in pieces with a wooden spoon; as soon as it is melted, add the fontina and the asiago cheeses repeating what you have done for the gorgonzola cheese. When all cheeses are melted, add the brandy and a pinch of pepper; let sauce cook for 2 minutes or so on a low fire. Generally it does not need any salt. If sauce is too thick, add a bit of milk mixed with the cream cheese. Cook the penne al dente, drain water, add the sauce, stir well and add the parmesan, always stirring. If you wish, you can sprinkle on the penne the chopped parsley. It adds a bit of color and the taste is good.

Serves 4.

EDOARDO LEBANO
Professor, French and Italian
IU Bloomington

Little Lamb Stew

2 1/2 pounds neck or lamb shank
2 carrots
1 stalk celery
small piece knob celery
1 medium onion
1 soft tomato
1/2 can tomato sauce
1/4 pound string beans
3 potatoes
spices (salt, garlic powder, pepper)

Cut up and put celery, carrot, onion, tomato and sauce into pot with 1/4 pot of water and a pinch of salt. Start cooking. While veggies are cooking, cut meat into large cubes. Put garlic powder, salt, pepper into brown bag (some people use flour). Add meat and coat. Place meat in a pan and sear a little until slightly brown, turn 3 or 4 times. Put meat into pot with veggies, water should nearly cover meat. Stir from time to time to check that veggies don't catch. Cook 3/4 hour and then add potatoes which have been cut into medium cubes (or smaller). Cook 1/4 hour more and add beans. Cook until tender. Serve either immediately or chill, de-fat and re-heat. (some people like to add dill (1/2 teaspoon) at last 15 minutes.

MIRIAM LANGSAM
Professor, History
IUPUI Indianapolis

Swedish Meatballs

1 medium onion
2 stalks celery
2 pounds ground chuck
2 eggs slightly beaten
2 cans bouillon undiluted
1 teaspoon poultry seasoning
1 teaspoon salt
1/4 teaspoon pepper
1 cup fine, dry bread crumbs
1/4 cup butter
2 cans cream of mushroom soup
1/2 teaspoon dill seed

Grind onion and celery (or mince finely) and mix with beef and eggs. Add 1/2 can bouillon, seasonings and bread crumbs. Roll into balls about l inch in diameter.

Brown in butter.

Blend remaining buillon, mushroom soup and dill; pour over meat balls and simmer 10 minutes.

Serve as hors d'oeuvres or over rice as a main dish.

MARGARET APPLEGATE
Professor, Nursing
IUPUI Indianapolis

One Pot Meal

2 pounds ground turkey
1 cup chopped onion
1/3 cup soy sauce
2 cups boiling water
1 can cream of mushroom soup
1/4 teaspoon garlic powder
1 8-ounce can mushrooms, drained
1/2 teaspoon salt (optional)
2 cups chopped celery
1 cup uncooked rice (not minute-type)

Brown meat and onions in a Dutch oven. Add remaining ingredients and stir to combine.

Bake at 350° for 1 hour or until celery is tender.

Cover pot for last half hour of baking.

Serves 6.

MARK E. WILLIAMS
Former Professor, Physics and Chemistry
IU Bloomington

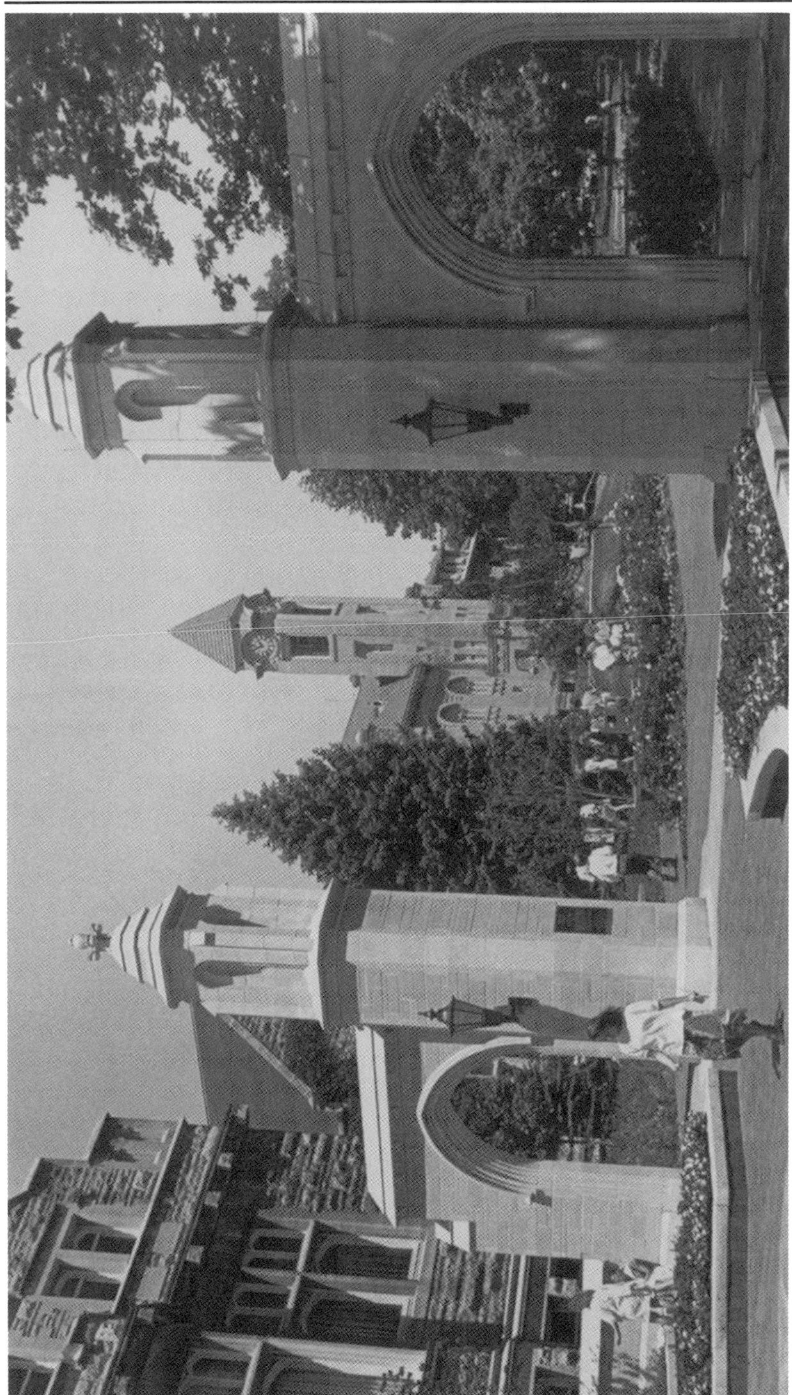

Home base—Bloomington!

Chicken Bake

In a 9 x 13-inch oven-safe dish, put 4 cups boiled, diced turkey or chicken pieces; stir 1 can cream of chicken and 1 can cream of celery soup and 1-8 ounces sour cream; pour over chicken.

On top of that, sprinkle 1 small package of packaged herb dressing. Combine 1 jar of prepared chicken gravy and 1 can chicken broth; Pour on top. Cut 1 stick of butter in pieces and add on top of mixture.

Bake at 350° for 50–60 minutes.

EARL BATES
Professor Emeritus, Music
IU Bloomington

"This dessert has become a tradition in my Early Childhood Education classes 'last evening fling.' It has been my secret recipe, but with retirement I bequeath it to IU."

—P.H.L.

Punch Bowl Cake

1 yellow cake
2 boxes instant pudding (vanilla or cream of coconut or lemon)
2 cans cherry pie filling
2 small cans crushed pineapple or 1 large can (drained)
5 bananas (ripe and firm)
2 cartons (12 ounces) whipped topping
1 cup pecans, chopped
maraschino cherries as garnish for top

This is two sets of layers, so divide each ingredient in half, layer the first half and then start over again and layer the rest of each ingredient. (NOTE: Recipe can be halved by using only one set of layers.)

In the bottom of a large punch bowl, crumble half of the cake. Pour over it one prepared pudding then 1 can of cherry filling, one small can or half of a large can of drained pineapple, 2 bananas, 1 carton of whipped topping, 1/2 cup pecans.

Crumble the rest of the cake and repeat the layers finishing with pecans and maraschino cherries on top of whipped topping.

Chill for at least 2 hours, or overnight. May be frozen and used immediately upon thawing. Serves 40.

P. HELEN LEWIS
Assistant Professor, Education
IU South Bend

Shrimp in Avocado Ring

Lemon wedges, to serve with the shrimp, make an appropriate garnish.

1 3-ounce package lemon flavored gelatin
1 cup mayonnaise or salad dressing
1 or 2 tablespoons lemon juice
1/2 teaspoon salt
2 medium avocados, peeled and sieved (1 cup)
1 cup whipping cream, whipped
lettuce
cleaned and cooked shrimp

Dissolve gelatin in 1 cup boiling water. Chill till partially set. Whip till fluffy. Stir in mayonnaise, lemon juice and salt. Fold in avocado and whipped cream.

Pour into 5 1/2 cup ring mold or six to eight 1/2-cup ring molds. Chill till firm. Unmold on lettuce, fill center with shrimp.

Makes 6 to 8 servings.

ASHTON VERAMALLAY
Associate Professor, Economics
IU East

Ratatouille

1 medium eggplant
1 tablespoon salt
1/4 cup olive oil
2 large onions
3 cloves garlic
2 green peppers (cut into strips)
4 medium zucchini (cut into bite sized pieces)
2 medium ripe tomatoes (cut into wedges)
1/4 teaspoon salt
ground black pepper
1/2 teaspoon thyme
1 bay leaf
2 tablespoons parsley finely chopped

Cut eggplant into thick slices, then into small pieces. Sprinkle with salt. Let stand 30 minutes then rinse and dry on paper towels. Heat oil in a large skillet. Saute onions and garlic (2 minutes). Add green pepper, cook 2 more minutes. Add eggplant, cook for 3 minutes, stirring constantly. Add zucchini, cook 3 minutes, then tomatoes, salt, ground black pepper, thyme, and bay leaf. Simmer uncovered for 40 minutes or until all vegetables are tender. Remove bay leaf.

Can be prepared ahead of time. Garnish with parsley and serve hot.

Can also be served cold as an appetizer or as a side dish on a picnic.

ANNE-MARIE POINSATTE
Associate Professor, French
IU South Bend

Bob's Guacamole

3 avocados, sliced
1 small onion, chopped
1 small tomato, chopped (optional)
1/3 cup chopped chiles
2 tablespoons lemon juice
2 tablespoons salsa (optional)
2 or 3 cloves garlic
1 to 2 tablespoons sugar
hot red pepper sauce to taste
salt to taste

Place all in large bowl, mash with potato masher until blended well. Do not overdo the mashing.

Serve with tortilla chips. Serves 6.

ROBERT JESKE
Associate Professor, Anthropology
IU Fort Wayne

Salmon and Green Bean Stew

water (just enough to cover vegetables)
4 cups green beans, fresh, frozen or canned
2 cups diced celery and leaves
4 medium potatoes, peeled and sliced thin
3 or 4 carrots, peeled and sliced thin
2 leeks, washed and sliced thin (use white, yellow-green, and almost all of green stalk)
1 clove garlic
salt and pepper to taste
seasoned salt to taste
12–16 ounces canned drained pink salmon
1 can evaporated milk
4 tablespoons chopped parsley or 1 tablespoon dried parsley
large pinch of rosemary

In large pot combine green beans, celery, potatoes, carrots, leeks, garlic, salt, pepper, season salt and cover with water. Simmer until vegetables are just tender. Add salmon and evaporated milk, parsley and rosemary.

Heat, don't boil, serve piping hot.

ELIZABETH M. LION
Associate Professor, Nursing
IU Bloomington

"Marvelous and splendid for people searching for low fat options. A winner every time—have recipe handy to distribute."

—E.M.L.

Greek Salad

2 medium iceberg lettuce, chopped
2 heads endive, chopped
4 tomatoes, peeled and chopped
1/2 cup pitted ripe black olives, sliced
1/2 cup sliced green onions
1 1/2 cups olive or salad oil
2/3 cup white wine vinegar
1 teaspoon salt
1/2 teaspoon oregano leaves
1/4 teaspoon pepper
1 1/2 cups feta cheese cubed or grated (6 ounces—I use any dry cheese)
4 ounces anchovies, drained (optional)

Toss together lettuce and endive. Arrange in individual salad plates. Arrange tomatoes, olives and onions on top of greens.

In screw top jar combine oil, vinegar, salt, oregano and pepper. Cover and shake to blend. Pour over salad.

Top each salad with cheese and anchovies.

Serves 8 (or put into one large bowl and serve individual portions)

ELIZABETH M. LION
Associate Professor, Nursing
IU Bloomington

Poppy Seed Cake

2 1/4 cup sifted flour
1 teaspoon salt
1/2 cup poppy seed
1 cup milk
4 egg whites or 2 eggs
4 teaspoons baking powder
1 1/2 cups sugar
1/2 cup shortening
1 teaspoon vanilla

Sift dry ingredients including sugar into a mixing bowl. Stir in poppy seed. Add shortening and 2/3 cup milk to dry ingredients. Beat for two minutes. Add unbeaten whites and remaining 1/3 cup milk, beat for two minutes more. The batter will be somewhat thin.

Bake in layers or in one cake pan at 350° for 30-35 minutes.

Cream Cheese Frosting for the Poppy Seed Cake

About 1/2 of pound box of powdered sugar (more or less to suit taste)
1 teaspoon vanilla
1 tablespoon butter or margarine
1 8-ounce package cream cheese

Let cream cheese and butter warm to room temperature. Mix together (I use a spoon; the mixer could be used—it's pretty gooey, but try if you want) Then add powdered sugar a little at a time, stir till well mixed. Add vanilla. Blend; spread on cool cake and ENJOY!

ELIZABETH M. LION
Associate Professor, Nursing
IU Bloomington

Company Chicken Casserole

5 cups cooked chicken
2 cans chicken noodle soup
2 cans cream of chicken soup
2 eggs, beaten
8 slices bread, cut into cubes
2 cups chicken broth
1 can sliced water chestnuts (if desired)
1 1/2 cups crushed Ritz crackers
1/4 cup margarine, melted

Mix all ingredients except crackers and margarine. Put into buttered 9 x 9-inch casserole. Mix crushed crackers and margarine, and sprinkle on top.

Bake at 350° for 1 hour.

Serves 6–8.

JANE VINCENT
Assistant Professor, Nursing
IU East

Delicious Turkey Meatloaf

(Especially good for those on heart diets)

1 pound lean ground turkey
1 cup packaged herb stuffing
1 cup beef broth
1 medium onion finely chopped
1/4 cup grated parmesan cheese
1/4 cup chopped parsley (optional)
1 tablespoon olive oil or margarine
Italian herbs to taste
Salt and pepper

Saute onion in oil. Add stuffing and moisten with beef broth. Mix in ground turkey and parmesan cheese. Season with Italian herbs and parsley, and light salt and pepper to taste. Add more or less broth to keep mixture very moist.

Shape into loaf; bake at 375° for 45 minutes.

Serves 4 generously.

KAREN SHAW
Professor, Music
IU Bloomington

French Loaf Spinach Dip

(Great for parties—pleasing to eye and palate)

1 package ranch salad dressing mix
2 cups (1 pint) sour cream
1 package (10 ounces) frozen chopped spinach, cooked and drained
1/4 cup onion, minced
3/4 teaspoon basil
1/2 teaspoon oregano

Combine all ingredients. Stir to blend. Chill for at least 1 hour. Serve in hollowed-out round loaf of french bread; use hollowed out section to make bread cubes for dipping.

TIMOTHY BALDWIN
Assistant Professor, Business Administration
IUPUI Indianapolis

Graduation—farewell, but never good-bye.

Index of Recipes

S

T

V

W

Z